DISCOVERIES IN SPACE SCIENCE

Shuttles and Space Missions

GENERAL EDITORS:
Giles Sparrow, Judith John,
and Chris McNab

Cavendish Square
New York

Published in 2016 by Cavendish Square Publishing, LLC
243 5th Avenue, Suite 136, New York, NY 10016

Website: cavendishsq.com

This publication represents the opinions and views of the author based on his or her personal experience, knowledge, and research. The information in this book serves as a general guide only. The author and publisher have used their best efforts in preparing this book and disclaim liability rising directly or indirectly from the use and application of this book.

CPSIA Compliance Information: Batch #CW16CSQ

All websites were available and accurate when this book was sent to press.

Cataloging-in-Publication Data

Sparrow, Giles.
Shuttles and space missions / edited by Giles Sparrow, Judith John, and Chris McNab.
p. cm. — (Discoveries in space science)
Includes index.
ISBN 978-1-5026-1016-4 (hardcover) ISBN 978-1-5026-1017-1 (ebook)
1. Astronautics — Juvenile literature. 2. Manned space flight — Juvenile literature. 3. Outer space — Exploration — Juvenile literature. I. Sparrow, Giles, 1970-. II. John, Judith. III. McNab, Chris, 1970-. IV. Title.
TL793.S63 2016
629.409—d23

Project Editor: Michael Spilling
Design: Hawes Design and Mark Batley
Picture Research: Terry Forshaw
Additional Text: Chris McNab and Judith John

All images are taken from the card set Secrets of the Universe (six volumes) published by International Masters Publishers AB, except the following: NASA/Tony Gray, Tom Farrar March 15, 2009, cover, 1; 3Dsculptor/Shutterstock.com, 4-5; Corbis: 51 (He Yuan/EPA), 52 top (Xinhua/Xinhua Press), 52 main (Lu Zhe/Xinhua Press), 52 bottom (Ren Junchuary/Xinhau Press).

Printed in the United States of America

TABLE OF CONTENTS

Shuttles and
Space Missions

MERCURY CRAFT

The late 1950s saw the start of the race between the US and the Soviet Union to launch a human being into orbit. In the interests of speed, both nations opted for systems based on a simple, recoverable nose cone that could be launched by an existing intercontinental ballistic missile. In the end, the Soviets won—with *Vostok 1* in April 1961. But America's Mercury capsule, which made its manned debut a month later, was a far more sophisticated craft and flew a total of six manned missions between 1961 and 1963.

MERCURY FLIGHT LOG

Mercury spacecraft manned flights 1961–3

Name	Mission	Launcher	Launch date	Duration	Crew	Flight
Freedom 7	MR-3	Redstone	May 5, 1961	15 min	Shepard	Suborbital
Liberty Bell 7	MR-4	Redstone	July 21, 1961	16 min	Grissom	Suborbital
Friendship 7	MA-6	Atlas	February 20, 1962	4 hr, 55 min	Glenn	Three orbits
Aurora 7	MA-7	Atlas	May 24, 1962	4 hr, 56 min	Carpenter	Three orbits
Sigma 7	MA-8	Atlas	October 3, 1962	9 hr, 13 min	Schirra	Six orbits
Faith 7	MA-9	Atlas	May 15, 1963	34 hr, 20 min	Cooper	22.5 orbits

MAN IN A CAN

Enclose the driver's seat of a small compact as far as the pedals, put on six layers of clothes, then enter feet-first through the sunroof and you have an idea of what it was like to squeeze into a Mercury capsule. Those who flew it said that you didn't climb into a Mercury, you put it on! To add to the discomfort, the forces on astronauts at launch reached 7 g and during reentry up to 11 g—eleven times their Earth weight.

Mercury's builders could not be sure how astronauts would react in space, so the craft was designed not to rely on them. The chief means of control was the onboard automatic stabilization and control system, which was monitored from the ground by a rate stabilization and control system. In emergencies, the astronaut could take over some of these functions—known as manual proportional control—and there was also a fully manual system.

Even so, an astronaut had only limited control over the capsule. He could align it from side to side or up and down, and roll it using eighteen hydrogen peroxide–powered thruster nozzles. But if anything major went wrong, there was little that he could do about it.

WINDOW ON THE WORLD

The display console included a revolving globe to show the astronaut his position as he orbited the Earth at 17,500 miles per hour (28,160 kmh). There was also a periscope system with a screen that displayed a black-and-white image of what lay immediately below. For the first Mercury astronaut, Alan Shepard, this was his only means of viewing the outside world. However, windows were fitted to all the subsequent capsules in the Mercury program.

At the base of the capsule was a pack of three solid-propellant retrorockets that could be manually fired as the astronaut aligned the craft at the correct angle for reentry. The pack was then discarded to expose an ablative—designed-to-melt—heat shield. This absorbed the searing 3,000 degrees Fahrenheit (1,600 degrees Celsius) heat of reentry, which occurred 25 miles (40 km) up, at a speed of 15,000 miles per hour (24,000 kmh).

Because the Mercury spacecrafts had a blunt shape and reentered base-down at a slight angle, they could generate enough lift to permit some aerodynamic control. By using the manual controls the astronaut could vary his flight path and hence the craft's point of splashdown in the ocean.

At an altitude of 10,000 feet (3,048 meters) and a speed of 400 miles per hour (644 kmh), a 63-foot (19 m)-diameter chute was deployed to slow the craft to about 20 miles per hour (32 kmh) at sea level. Just before splashdown, an airbag inflated under the heat shield to cushion the impact.

LUCKY 7

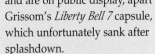

Alan Shepard named his spacecraft *Freedom* and added the number 7 because it was the craft's factory production number. Gus Grissom, who flew the next mission, named his craft *Liberty Bell* He, too, added the number 7, partly because Shepard had, but also because he thought it would be a good way to commemorate the seven astronauts in the Mercury Program. The other astronauts followed suit: *Friendship 7* (John Glenn), *Aurora 7* (Scott Carpenter), *Sigma 7* (Walter Schirra), and *Faith 7* (Gordon Cooper). Grounded astronaut Deke Slayton was going to name his capsule *Delta 7*.

WHERE ARE THEY NOW?

...THE MERCURY CAPSULES

Anyone looking at one of the surviving Mercury capsules will readily appreciate the courage of the astronauts who flew them.

Although the Soviet Union had already launched a successful manned spacecraft, the physical and psychological effects of spaceflight were still largely unknown when the manned Mercury flights began. The Mercury successes proved that manned spaceflight was not as dangerous to the body as many believed.

The biggest fears were that weightlessness would result in severe disorientation and that the stress of the g-forces during reentry would cause injury. There were also concerns that space travelers would be psychologically affected. These fears were largely dispelled by the success of Mercury. Even so, with space technology in its infancy, the risks were still enormous. The launch vehicles were no more than lightly modified guided missiles. And the capsules were equally crude by modern standards. The tiny conical section in which the astronaut traveled was just 6 feet 10 inches (2 m) long by 6 feet 2.5 inches (1.9 m) at its widest point.

Of the six manned Mercury capsules, five have been preserved and are on public display, apart from Gus Grissom's *Liberty Bell 7* capsule, which unfortunately sank after splashdown.

MERCURY CAPSULE

heat shield

pressurized inner capsule

titanium/nickel alloy outer shell

ceramic fiber insulation

retrorocket pack

control stick

reentry parachutes

control thrusters

periscope

antennae and infrared horizon sensors

escape rocket nozzles

aerodynamic spike

PRESSURE SUIT
The cabin atmosphere was 100 percent pure oxygen, and the astronaut wore a pressure suit with a helmet. The helmet's visor could be opened so that the astronaut could take a drink or eat bite-sized chunks of food.

ESCAPE system
The orange-painted nose-mounted launch escape rocket (right) was designed to fire and pull the Mercury capsule to safety in case the launch vehicle malfunctioned either during or immediately after launch.

Alan Shepard's capsule is on display at the National Air and Space Museum.

CONTROLS
Aside from limited manual takeover in an emergency, the astronaut had very little control of the craft. Most of the displays were for monitoring.

VOSTOK MISSIONS

The Soviet Union stunned the world in 1957 with the launch of *Sputnik 1*, the Earth's first artificial satellite. By 1961, they were ready to extend their lead in the Space Race. Under the brilliant leadership of Sergei Korolev, Soviet engineers built the Vostok craft, designed to take a person into space. And on April 12, 1961, it did just that—Yuri Gagarin orbited the Earth in 108 minutes. Five missions later, Valentina Tereshkova became the first woman in orbit. The pioneering age of spaceflight had truly begun.

VOSTOK MISSION FACTS

Craft	Cosmonaut	Date	Orbits	Duration
V1	Yuri Gagarin	April 12, 1961	1	1 hr 48 min
V2	Gherman Titov	August 6, 1961	17	1 day 1 hr 18min
V3	Andrian Nikolayev	August 11, 1962	64	3 days 22 hr 22 min
V4	Pavel Popovich	August 12, 1962	48	2 days 22 hr 57 min
V5	Valery Bykovsky	June 14, 1963	81	4 days 23 hr 6 min
V6	Valentina Tereshkova	June 16, 1963	48	2 days 22 hr 50 min

STARS OF THE EAST

Fifteen minutes into Yuri Gagarin's historic flight aboard *Vostok 1*, a monitoring post off Alaska detected what sounded like a conversation between the Baikonur Cosmodrome in Soviet Kazakhstan and a spacecraft in Earth orbit. For once, the usually secretive Soviets were happy to be overheard. Months earlier, US President John F. Kennedy had declared: "If the Soviet Union were first in outer space, that would be the most serious defeat the United States has suffered in many, many years." Now, his words would come back to haunt him.

If *Vostok 1* was a political victory for the Kremlin, it was a personal triumph for Sergei Korolev and his team at Baikonur. Korolev had survived Stalinist purges, the Nazi invasion of Russia, and many other setbacks in his drive to build a workable spacecraft. As a new decade dawned, it was only a matter of time before one carried a cosmonaut into space. But who would it be?

The two leading contenders were Gagarin and Gherman Titov. Korolev chose the smiling Gagarin—the model of a communist hero. But Titov's *Vostok 2* mission was another great leap forward—seventeen orbits and a full day in space. The American response came in February 1962, with John Glenn's three orbits aboard *Friendship 7*.

MISSION DIARY: *VOSTOK 1–6*

July 1958
Sergei Korolev outlines the advantages of Vostok missions in letter to Soviet leaders.
November 1958
Vostok program approved.
March 1960
Twenty cosmonauts (including Gherman Titov, right) begin intensive training for Vostok flights.
August 19, 1960
Test of Vostok launch vehicle with two dogs, Belka and Strelka, aboard. It is successfully recovered.
March 9, 1961
Successful recovery of a Vostok craft with a dog, Chernushka, aboard.
March 25, 1961
Final test launch. Canine passenger Zvezdochka (right) recovered safely.
April 12, 1961
First human spaceflight. Yuri Gagarin orbits Earth aboard *Vostok 1*.

August 6, 1961
Vostok 2 cosmonaut Titov (right) completes a full day in space.
February 20, 1962
US puts a man in orbit—John Glenn, aboard *Friendship 7*.
August 11, 1962
Joint mission of *Vostok 3* and *4*. Cosmonauts Andrian Nikolayev and Pavel Popovich pass within just over 3 miles (5 km) of each other in orbit.
August 12
Popovich (right) in *Vostok 4* is brought back a day early after ground control misinterprets some of his comments as being code words for a problem.
June 14–16, 1963
Joint mission of *Vostok 5* and *6*. *Vostok 5* fails to reach the correct orbit for rendezvous and its mission is cut short. *Vostok 6* makes history, as Valentina Tereshkova becomes the first woman in space.

Yet within months, the Soviets surged ahead again when *Vostok 3* and *4*, launched twenty-four hours apart, passed within 3 miles (5 km) of each other in the first space rendezvous.

Vostok 5 and *6* were also paired in June 1963, giving Korolev the chance to show that docking two spacecraft in orbit was within his reach. But the Soviets' biggest success was in the propaganda war. In *Vostok 6* was a woman—Valentina Tereshkova.

SIGN OF HONOR

One of the highlights of a cosmonaut's career is the ceremonial signing of Yuri Gagarin's diary. This tradition was initiated as a tribute to the "First Cosmonaut" after he was killed in a plane crash in 1968. Here, Mir 18 cosmonaut Vladimir Dezhurov signs, watched by guest NASA astronaut Norman Thagard (seated left). The two men had recently returned from Mir aboard the Shuttle *Atlantis*, after the first Mir–Shuttle docking in 1995.

MISSION PROFILE

1 LIFTOFF
Vostok 1 blasted off from the Baikonur Cosmodrome in Soviet Kazakhstan atop a modified R-7 intercontinental ballistic missile containing no fewer than thirty-two thrust chambers. Once in orbit, the shields protecting the two-module spacecraft were discarded.

2 ORBIT
Gagarin sat upright in a modified pilot's ejection seat in the spherical crew module. This was supplied with power and a pressurized oxygen/nitrogen mixture by the equipment module. The orbit lasted 89 minutes.

3 REENTRY
Retrorocket fired to brake the craft, then explosive bolts released the equipment module. The crew module plunged into the atmosphere, protected from the heat of air friction by an ablative shield, which was designed to burn off during reentry. At an altitude of 4.5 miles (7 km) above the Soviet Union, Gagarin ejected.

BAD NEWS

It was 3:30 a.m. in Florida when Moscow radio broadcast the news that Gagarin had circled the Earth. When telephoned by reporters for a comment, a shocked and angry Colonel John "Shorty" Powers, press officer for NASA's Mercury program, came up with the unfortunate response: "We're all asleep down here!"

GEMINI
1 AND *2*

Without the Gemini program, there would have been no Apollo. It was NASA's twelve Gemini missions that bridged the gap between single-person and multi-crew spacecraft and grappled with the technical problems of sending astronauts to the Moon. But before the twin-seat Gemini capsule could undertake crewed missions, its technology had to be rigorously tested. *Gemini 1* and *2* verified that the new spacecraft was safe enough to send two people into orbit—and get them back again.

GEMINI DATA

	GEMINI 1	*GEMINI 2*
CREW	NONE	NONE
LAUNCH VEHICLE	TITAN 2	TITAN 2
LAUNCH WEIGHT	3.51 TONS (3.18 METRIC TONS)	3.43 TONS (3.11 T)
LAUNCH DATE	APRIL 8, 1964	JANUARY 19, 1965
LAUNCH COMPLEX	PAD 19, CAPE KENNEDY	PAD 19, CAPE KENNEDY
MISSION	3 PLANNED ORBITS (BUT LASTED FOR 64)	18-MINUTE SUBORBITAL FLIGHT
TEST GOALS	LAUNCHER, LAUNCHER/SPACECRAFT COMPATIBILITY	ALL SYSTEMS, HEAT SHIELD, RECOVERY
HIGHEST ALTITUDE	200 MILES (321 KM)	107 MILES (172 KM)
RECOVERY DATE	NOT RECOVERED; BURNED UP APRIL 12, 1964	JANUARY 19, 1964, IN SOUTH ATLANTIC

MACHINE BEFORE MAN

The first two Gemini flights thundered off the launchpad in April 1964 and January 1965 without crew. In their place were instruments to record temperature, vibration, g force, and other factors—and help make sure future launches were safe for astronauts.

Gemini 1, sitting atop its equally new two-stage Titan 2 launcher, reached space safely and was tracked as it orbited the Earth. Four days and sixty-four orbits after leaving Cape Kennedy, it burned up as planned over the South Atlantic Ocean. Now NASA knew that their new spacecraft could fly. *Gemini 2*'s job was to determine whether it could return astronauts in one piece.

Gemini 2's flight was planned as a short, suborbital mission—a ballistic hop, similar to Alan Shepard's *Freedom 7* flight, that would test all systems from launch to splashdown. After four weather-related delays and one false start, *Gemini 2* was finally launched successfully on its 18-minute flight. The first and second stages of the Titan launcher separated without a hitch, and soon the capsule was firing its retrorockets to begin the return to Earth. *Gemini 2* was programmed to shoot through the atmosphere at much higher speeds than later flights to test its heat shield. It survived and splashed into the ocean, suspended from its single parachute.

The way was now clear for more complex crewed missions. Two months after *Gemini 2*, astronauts Gus Grissom and John Young entered Earth orbit aboard *Gemini 3* to practice the spaceflight techniques that would one day be used to land men on the Moon.

MISSION DIARY: *GEMINI 1* AND *2*

GEMINI 1
MAY 21, 1963
GEMINI'S BRAND-NEW TITAN LAUNCHER IS COMPLETED.
JULY 5, 1963
TESTING OF *GEMINI 1* BEGINS.
OCTOBER 4, 1963
GEMINI 1 IS DELIVERED TO CAPE KENNEDY IN FLORIDA.
MARCH 3, 1964
GEMINI 1 IS PLACED ON LAUNCHPAD.
APRIL 8, 1964
GEMINI 1 IS LAUNCHED (ABOVE).

APRIL 12, 1964
AFTER A TOTAL OF SIXTY-FOUR ORBITS, *GEMINI 1* BURNS UP ON REENTRY.
GEMINI 2
AUG-SEP 1964
HURRICANES DELAY *GEMINI 2*'S LAUNCH. ITS LAUNCHER IS REMOVED FROM THE LAUNCHPAD.
SEPTEMBER 21, 1964
THE *GEMINI 2* CAPSULE ARRIVES AT CAPE KENNEDY. THE LAUNCH IS RESCHEDULED FOR LATE FALL.
OCTOBER 18, 1964
GEMINI 2 IS DISPATCHED TO THE LAUNCHPAD.

NOVEMBER 28, 1964
FINAL TESTS ON THE SPACECRAFT AND LAUNCHER ARE COMPLETED.
DECEMBER 9, 1964
SECONDS AFTER THE TITAN LAUNCHER'S ENGINES IGNITE, THE LAUNCH IS AUTOMATICALLY HALTED.
JANUARY 19, 1965
ON ITS SECOND ATTEMPT, *GEMINI 2* LAUNCHES (LEFT). DURING ITS 2,000-MILE (3,218 KM) JOURNEY, AN ONBOARD CAMERA BELOW ITS THRUSTERS TAKES THE PICTURE OF EARTH (ABOVE).

TWIN TEST MISSIONS

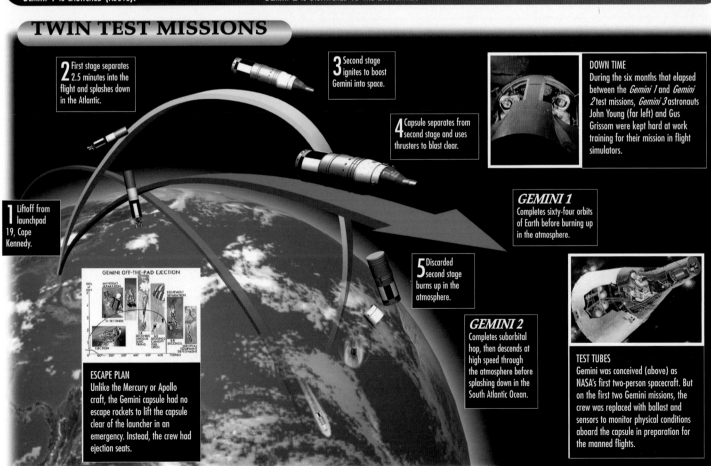

2 First stage separates 2.5 minutes into the flight and splashes down in the Atlantic.

3 Second stage ignites to boost Gemini into space.

4 Capsule separates from second stage and uses thrusters to blast clear.

DOWN TIME
During the six months that elapsed between the *Gemini 1* and *Gemini 2* test missions, *Gemini 3* astronauts John Young (far left) and Gus Grissom were kept hard at work training for their mission in flight simulators.

1 Liftoff from launchpad 19, Cape Kennedy.

GEMINI 1
Completes sixty-four orbits of Earth before burning up in the atmosphere.

5 Discarded second stage burns up in the atmosphere.

ESCAPE PLAN
Unlike the Mercury or Apollo craft, the Gemini capsule had no escape rockets to lift the capsule clear of the launcher in an emergency. Instead, the crew had ejection seats.

GEMINI 2
Completes suborbital hop, then descends at high speed through the atmosphere before splashing down in the South Atlantic Ocean.

TEST TUBES
Gemini was conceived (above) as NASA's first two-person spacecraft. But on the first two Gemini missions, the crew was replaced with ballast and sensors to monitor physical conditions aboard the capsule in preparation for the manned flights.

THE FIRST SPACEWALK

On March 18, 1965, *Voskhod 2* cosmonaut Alexei Leonov crawled into an 8-foot (2.4 m) air lock tunnel far above the Earth. He floated out of the other end into open space, to hurtle around the planet as continents and clouds passed below. The spacewalk was the last Soviet space spectacular, carried out in haste to upstage the US Gemini missions. Leonov's orbital adventure was risky and he was lucky to get back into his spacecraft alive. But survive he did—to go down in history as the first human to walk in space.

VOSKHOD 2 MISSION

SPACECRAFT	VOSKHOD 2, THE WORLD'S FOURTEENTH CREWED SPACEFLIGHT AND THE EIGHTH FROM THE SOVIET UNION	AIRLOCK DIMENSIONS	4 FT X 8 FT 4 IN (1.2 x 2.5M)
		AIRLOCK MASS	551 LB (250 KG)
		SPACEWALK DURATION	24 MINUTES OUTSIDE CAPSULE, WITH 12 MINUTES SPENT OUTSIDE AIR LOCK IN OPEN SPACE
LAUNCH	MARCH 18, 1965, FROM THE BAIKONUR COSMODROME		
CREW	PAVEL BELYAYEV AND ALEXEI LEONOV	MISSION DURATION	1 DAY 2 HR 2 MIN
		LANDING	MARCH 19, 1965, IN NORTHERN RUSSIA
MAXIMUM ALTITUDE	310 MILES (499 KM)		
SPEED	17,400 MPH (28,000 KMH)		

RISKY VENTURE

Cold War officials in the Soviet Union made cosmonaut Alexei Leonov's first historic steps in space sound like a walk in the park. A government news agency reported that Leonov "felt well" during his swim in space and on his return to the *Voskhod 2* capsule. Leonov apparently enjoyed good control over his movements thanks to a 50-foot (15 m) tether. To the US government and the world at large, the first spacewalk was presented as an easy triumph for Soviet engineering.

In reality, Leonov had been doing anything but enjoying the view during his 24-minute space adventure on March 18, 1965. He nearly suffered heat stroke as he somersaulted around space and spent several fraught minutes struggling to reenter *Voskhod 2*. Leonov has since revealed that he carried a suicide pill in case commander Pavel Belyayev was forced to leave him in orbit.

The politics of the Cold War made it vital to paint Leonov's maneuver as a total success. With the Gemini program, the US threatened to seize the lead in the Space Race, and the Soviets were determined to meet or beat Gemini's goals, one of which was the first spacewalk. At short notice and with Soyuz still under development, Soviet engineers had to work with what they had. In the end, Leonov exited a modified Vostok capsule based on the design that took Yuri Gagarin to another first—first person in orbit—in 1961. *Voskhod 2* was fitted with a Volga inflatable air lock to maintain cabin pressures and prepare Leonov for his spacewalk.

HUMAN SATELLITE

Leonov entered the air lock tunnel through *Voskhod 2*'s hatch 300 miles (500 km) above the Pacific Ocean. There was a short wait while the air lock pressure was lowered to the space vacuum—if the pressures had not been equalized Leonov would have shot out like a cork from a bottle. As the air lock opened, Leonov floated headfirst into space.

The conditions inside Leonov's spacesuit recreated a little Earth atmosphere, with steady temperature and the correct levels of breathing gases. But without the luxury of gravity, Leonov found it hard to control the cord that tied him to *Voskhod 2*. After a poorly

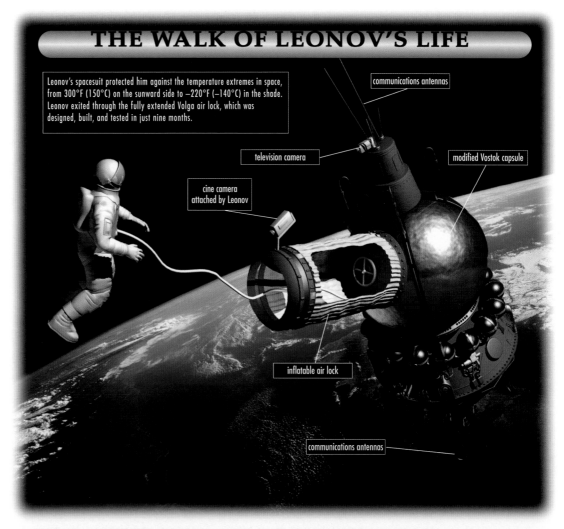

THE WALK OF LEONOV'S LIFE

Leonov's spacesuit protected him against the temperature extremes in space, from 300°F (150°C) on the sunward side to −220°F (−140°C) in the shade. Leonov exited through the fully extended Volga air lock, which was designed, built, and tested in just nine months.

communications antennas

modified Vostok capsule

television camera

cine camera attached by Leonov

inflatable air lock

communications antennas

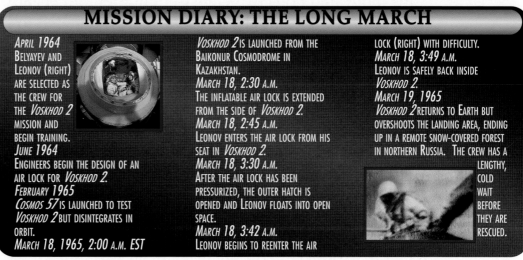

MISSION DIARY: THE LONG MARCH

APRIL 1964
BELYAYEV AND LEONOV (RIGHT) ARE SELECTED AS THE CREW FOR THE *VOSKHOD 2* MISSION AND BEGIN TRAINING.
JUNE 1964
ENGINEERS BEGIN THE DESIGN OF AN AIR LOCK FOR *VOSKHOD 2*.
FEBRUARY 1965
COSMOS 57 IS LAUNCHED TO TEST *VOSKHOD 2* BUT DISINTEGRATES IN ORBIT.
MARCH 18, 1965, 2:00 A.M. EST

VOSKHOD 2 IS LAUNCHED FROM THE BAIKONUR COSMODROME IN KAZAKHSTAN.
MARCH 18, 2:30 A.M.
THE INFLATABLE AIR LOCK IS EXTENDED FROM THE SIDE OF *VOSKHOD 2*.
MARCH 18, 2:45 A.M.
LEONOV ENTERS THE AIR LOCK FROM HIS SEAT IN *VOSKHOD 2*.
MARCH 18, 3:30 A.M.
AFTER THE AIR LOCK HAS BEEN PRESSURIZED, THE OUTER HATCH IS OPENED AND LEONOV FLOATS INTO OPEN SPACE.
MARCH 18, 3:42 A.M.
LEONOV BEGINS TO REENTER THE AIR

LOCK (RIGHT) WITH DIFFICULTY.
MARCH 18, 3:49 A.M.
LEONOV IS SAFELY BACK INSIDE *VOSKHOD 2*.
MARCH 19, 1965
VOSKHOD 2 RETURNS TO EARTH BUT OVERSHOOTS THE LANDING AREA, ENDING UP IN A REMOTE SNOW-COVERED FOREST IN NORTHERN RUSSIA. THE CREW HAS A LENGTHY, COLD WAIT BEFORE THEY ARE RESCUED.

timed pull, Leonov crashed into the spacecraft, rocking his comrade.

Leonov spent 12 minutes floating freely in space before he was instructed to reenter the air lock. But with his spacesuit inflated like a balloon, Leonov could not bend his legs enough to climb back into the air lock. After several attempts, Leonov was forced to bleed some of the suit's air to make it less rigid. In doing so, he risked a dangerous attack of the bends. With his pulse

racing, Leonov finally squeezed himself back into the air lock and closed the outer hatch. He was close to suffering heat stroke and reported that he was "up to the knees" in sweat.

More trouble awaited on Earth. A malfunction in *Voskhod 2*'s systems forced Belyayev to make a manually controlled descent. The spacecraft overshot its designated landing site by over 700 miles (1,100 km), to land in a remote, snowy forest in

northern Russia. The cosmonauts shivered for over two hours before a rescue helicopter arrived.

Whatever the difficulties, Leonov had made a landmark achievement—and most importantly, beaten US astronaut Ed White to the first spacewalk by three months. Although the US regained supremacy with the Apollo Moon landing and Neil Armstrong's giant leap, the first steps belong to Leonov.

THE PIONEERS

The first space travelers were dogs and chimpanzees. The very first living creature in orbit was the USSR's Laika, a husky cross stray found on a Moscow street. She survived four days aboard *Sputnik 2*, only the second craft to enter orbit, before running out of oxygen. The first human in space was cosmonaut Yuri Gagarin, who made just one orbit of the Earth in April 1961. American efforts to catch up began more cautiously, with Alan Shepard making a suborbital flight in May 1961 before John Glenn became the first US astronaut in orbit in February 1962. The so-called "Mercury 7" astronauts all flew in space solo before the more ambitious two-crew Gemini program began, followed by the three-man Apollo missions that culminated in the Moon landings and Neil Armstrong's first steps on the surface of another world.

The Space Shuttle fleet was retired in 2011. Although the Space Shuttle may have seemed to be a mature, rather than a pioneering space vehicle, it required more piloting skills than earlier spacecraft. US astronauts have traditionally come from military test pilot backgrounds, until recently ruling out female commanders. Eileen Collins became the first woman to command a US space mission in 1999 and was chosen to pilot the first Shuttle to fly following the 2003 *Columbia* disaster, confirming that the "right stuff" is not just a male attribute.

YURI GAGARIN

My God, he's got two daughters, how did he decide to do that? He must be crazy!" On April 12, 1961, these were the words with which Zoya Gagarin greeted the news that her brother Yuri had become the first man in space. Elsewhere, the reaction was more positive. Idolized by the world press, Yuri Gagarin became an icon of Soviet achievement. Gagarin died in 1968 after his personal life and career had become troubled, but he still remains respected as one of the great pioneers of space exploration.

LIFE LINES: YURI GAGARIN

FULL NAME	YURI ALEXEYEVICH GAGARIN		FAMILY	MARRIED VALYA (VALENTINA) GORYACHEVA 1957; TWO DAUGHTERS
DATE OF BIRTH	MARCH 9, 1934			
PLACE OF BIRTH	KLUSHINO, RUSSIA		CAREER	TRAINEE ORENBURG PILOT'S SCHOOL 1955–7; FIGHTER PILOT, BASED NEAR MURMANSK 1957–9; COSMONAUT 1961; DEPUTY DIRECTOR OF THE COSMONAUT TRAINING CENTER AT STAR CITY 1963–7; TEST PILOT 1968
EDUCATION	PRIMARY AND SECONDARY SCHOOLS IN KLUSHINO AND GZHATSK; APPRENTICE AT MOSCOW'S LYUBERTSY STEEL PLANT 1950–1; STUDENT OF TRACTOR CONSTRUCTION AT THE SARATOV TECHNICAL SCHOOL 1951–5			
			DATE OF DEATH	MARCH 27, 1968

Gagarin's flight will stir people's imaginations as long as the Earth exists.

SOVIET WRITER KONSTANTIN PAUSTOVKSI

Gagarin was the first man in space (above) on April 12, 1961. His capsule, the *Vostok 1* (center), was designed by Sergei Korolev and his team. After his record flight, he was treated as a hero, awarded medals (right), and honored by Soviet leader Nikita Khrushchev (top right).

Gagarin and his family became icons of Soviet progress (above center) and his untimely death sent millions into mourning. His state funeral (above) was one of the biggest ever seen in Moscow.

PEOPLE'S HERO

On October 4, 1957, the Soviet Union launched the world's first artificial satellite. Two years later the Soviets decided to replicate their triumph—but this time the satellite would carry a human being. From a list of 2,200 eager applicants for the honor of becoming the first cosmonaut, a shortlist of just 20 men was selected for further training. Among these men was a twenty-five-year-old fighter pilot named Yuri Gagarin.

Born on March 9, 1934, Yuri Gagarin was not an obvious choice of cosmonaut. A farmworker's son from Smolensk, he had survived the German occupation of World War II and had trained as a foundry apprentice before joining tractor school in 1951. On graduation he had progressed to the Soviet air force, where he proved himself an enthusiastic MiG pilot with a taste for heavy g-forces.

Gagarin was shorter than average—he needed to sit on a cushion to get a clear view over the

nose of his MiG—and had open, cheerful features. He married young and by the age of twenty-five he was already a father, living with his new family in standard Soviet military housing. Gagarin was unassuming, uncomplaining, and optimistic. In short, he was a textbook example of a Soviet citizen.

Gagarin's flying experience had little to do with his inclusion on the shortlist. He had spent 252 hours and 21 minutes in the air. Of these, only 75 hours had been as a solo pilot. Other candidates had been

airborne for some 1,500 hours. Instead, the selectors were swayed by his solid background, determination, and, most prosaically, by his size—the *Vostok 1* capsule in which the successful cosmonaut would travel had very little legroom.

ROCKET RIDE TO FAME

By the end of 1960, the twenty-man squad had been whittled down to six. And by the following April there were two favorites: Gagarin and an equally short pilot named Gherman Titov. After an examination of each man's abilities and his ideological soundness—Titov sported a suspiciously bourgeois hairstyle—the decision was reached on April 7, 1961. Five days later, Gagarin hurtled into space and completed a 108-minute orbit of the Earth.

On his return he was showered with honors. A publicist's dream, he smiled photogenically, talked simply but expressively, and charmed heads of state around the world. Such was his popularity that a special department was created to handle his fan mail.

Fame took its toll, however. On October 3, 1961, he incurred severe head injuries by jumping from a second-floor window in a Crimean resort. Officially, he had hurt himself rescuing his daughter from the Black Sea. In fact, his wife had found him with another woman.

Gagarin continued to work on the space program, but his advisory capacities were nullified by rapid leaps in technology. And in 1967, when he criticized the disastrous launch of a Soyuz spacecraft—he had been backup to the man who died aboard it—he was relieved of duties. He returned to the air force and died in a plane crash in 1968. Ironically, he had been flying with an instructor. He left behind a widow and two daughters.

CAREER TIMELINE

1934 Born in the village of Klushino located 100 miles (160 km) west of Moscow.
1951 After a year's apprenticeship at Moscow's Lyubertsy Steel Plant, enrolls in the Saratov Technical School to study tractor construction.
1955 On graduation joins the Orenburg Pilot's School, making his first MiG solo flight on March 26, 1957.
1957 Marries Valya Goryacheva. The following month graduates from Orenburg and is posted to Nikel airbase near Murmansk.

1960 Along with nineteen other would-be cosmonauts, Gagarin is transferred to the Star City space base, 30 miles (48 km) northeast of Moscow.
April 12, 1961 Chosen as the world's first cosmonaut only five days previously, Gagarin becomes the first man in space. His colleague, Gherman Titov, makes the second Soviet spaceflight a few months later.
April 14, 1961 A rapturous reception from Khrushchev inaugurates several years as a national hero.

1963 To keep Gagarin out of trouble, he is appointed Deputy Director of the Cosmonaut Training Center at Star City.
1967 Criticizes authorities when a Soyuz spacecraft crashes, killing its occupant, and is dismissed from the space team.
1968 Not having flown for five months, Gagarin takes off with an instructor in a MiG-15. The plane crashes in poor weather. Gagarin is identified by a birthmark on a scrap of flesh from the back of his neck and then given a hero's funeral.

JOHN GLENN

n 1962, wartime fighter pilot John Glenn became the first American to orbit the Earth. His dramatic mission made him an international hero, but his newfound fame put a stop to his career as an astronaut. President Kennedy grounded him, believing that if Glenn died, the public would turn against the US space program. But Glenn always believed that one day he would travel into space again, and thirty-six years later his belief was vindicated. In 1998, at age seventy-seven, he became the oldest man in space.

LIFE LINES

FULL NAME	JOHN HERSCHEL GLENN, JR.
DATE OF BIRTH	JULY 18, 1921
PLACE OF BIRTH	CAMBRIDGE, OHIO
EDUCATION	PRIMARY AND SECONDARY SCHOOLS IN NEW CONCORD, OHIO; MUSKINGUM COLLEGE, NEW CONCORD. BACHELOR OF SCIENCE IN ENGINEERING, PLUS NINE HONORARY DOCTORAL DEGREES
FAMILY	MARRIED ANNA MARGARET CASTOR, 1943; TWO CHILDREN, JOHN DAVID AND CAROLYN ANN, AND TWO GRANDCHILDREN
CAREER	US MARINES PILOT AND INSTRUCTOR 1943–56; TEST PILOT 1956–9; NASA ASTRONAUT AND SPACECRAFT ENGINEER 1959–64; BUSINESS EXECUTIVE 1965–74; ELECTED US SENATOR 1974–98; PAYLOAD SPECIALIST, SHUTTLE MISSION STS-95 OCTOBER 1998

SPACE SENATOR

By the winter of 1961, the United States was losing the Space Race—the bitterly contested battle for space supremacy being fought between the US and the Soviet Union. That spring, Soviet cosmonaut Yuri Gagarin had become the first person to orbit the Earth. Several months later, after a triumphant seventeen-orbit space flight by Soviet cosmonaut Gherman Titov, the score was: Soviet Union eighteen crewed orbits, US none.

These Soviet successes sent NASA scrambling to catch up, and on February 20, 1962, millions of people watched the television coverage of a 95-foot (29 m) Mercury-Atlas launch vehicle shooting into the sky and out of sight. The rocket's Mercury space capsule, *Friendship 7*, circled the Earth three times before reentering the atmosphere and landing in the Atlantic Ocean near Grand Turk Island, West Indies.

The occupant of the tiny capsule was Lieutenant-Colonel John H. Glenn, Jr., a US Marine Corps pilot who had joined the NASA Space Task Group in 1959. Glenn, born in Cambridge, Ohio, on July 18, 1921, saw action as a fighter pilot in both World War II and the Korean War and went on to became a test pilot.

Scheduled for no further space flights after his historic Mercury mission, Glenn left NASA in 1964 and spent most of the next decade as a businessman. In 1974, he was elected to represent Ohio in the Senate. On Capitol Hill, Glenn took a strong interest in environmental issues and his technical expertise was often called upon when he served on committees, including the Senate Armed Forces Committee. He was elected to the Senate a record fourth consecutive time in 1992.

A THIRTY-SIX-YEAR WAIT

For years, Senator Glenn lobbied for his own return to space and

Too often people set their lives by the calendar. It takes the fun out of life.
JOHN GLENN

Friendship 7 (top) lifts off with John Glenn on board. He returned to Earth a national hero, which helped him launch a career as a senator (top left). *Discovery* (top center) blasts off in October 1998. On board, Glenn takes a picture of Earth (center). Before takeoff, his wife Annie snaps a photo of Glenn (above).

US President Bill Clinton samples some of Glenn's space food (left). Glenn and his wife Annie (above) pose after his historic second spaceflight.

in 1998 his persistence finally paid off. NASA administrator Dan Goldin called Glenn "the most tenacious man alive" when he signed up the seventy-seven-year-old for the Shuttle mission STS-95 that fall.

On board the *Discovery*, Glenn found that NASA technology had come a long way since his last flight in the the 1960s. During takeoff, he experienced less than half the gravitational force that he had

on *Friendship 7*, and he also had far more room in which to move around.

As the oldest astronaut ever, Glenn once again served as an orbiting guinea pig. Weightlessness affects the human body much as old age does, for example, with a loss of bone mass. Glenn, now going through both at once, wore an electrode cap while asleep to monitor his brainwaves, and had blood samples taken by fellow astronauts. The data

collected was used in an ongoing study by the National Institutes of Health into the effects of aging.

But in one way, at least, thirty-six years haven't aged the hero. A day into the flight, *Discovery* commander Curtis Brown observed, "Let the record show that John has a smile on his face and it goes from one ear to the other one, and we haven't been able to remove it yet." Glenn and the other crewmembers landed safely eight days later.

CAREER TIMELINE

1942 RECEIVES DEGREE IN ENGINEERING FROM MUSKINGUM COLLEGE, NEW CONCORD, OHIO.
1942 ENTERS NAVAL AVIATION CADET PROGRAM.
1943 ENLISTS IN THE MARINE CORPS.
1943–5 DURING WW2, GLENN FLIES FIFTY-NINE COMBAT MISSIONS IN F-4U FIGHTER PLANES.
1948–50 ADVANCED FLIGHT INSTRUCTOR IN CORPUS CHRISTI, TEXAS.
1950–3 IN THE KOREAN WAR, GLENN FLIES A FURTHER NINETY COMBAT MISSIONS. GLENN HAS SIX DISTINGUISHED FLYING CROSSES AND THE AIR MEDAL WITH EIGHTEEN CLUSTERS FOR HIS SERVICE IN TWO WARS.

1957 FLIES AN F-8U CRUSADER FROM LOS ANGELES TO NEW YORK IN A RECORD TIME OF 3 HOURS 23 MINUTES. THIS IS THE FIRST TRANSCONTINENTAL FLIGHT TO AVERAGE ABOVE THE SPEED OF SOUND.
1956–9 HELPS DESIGN FIGHTER PLANES AT US NAVY BUREAU OF AERONAUTICS.
1959 CHOSEN WITH SIX OTHERS (CARPENTER, COOPER, GRISSOM, SCHIRRA, SHEPARD, AND SLAYTON) AS A MERCURY ASTRONAUT.
FEBRUARY 20, 1962 GLENN FLIES ON *MERCURY 6*, MAKING THE FIRST AMERICAN ORBITAL FLIGHT AND BECOMING THE FIFTH PERSON IN SPACE. HE MAKES THREE

ORBITS.
1964 RESIGNS FROM SPACE PROGRAM.
1974 BECOMES US SENATOR FOR OHIO.
OCTOBER 29, 1998 RETURNS TO SPACE ON BOARD *DISCOVERY* AS A PAYLOAD SPECIALIST.
NOVEMBER 7, 1998 RETURNS TO EARTH ON *DISCOVERY* (ABOVE) AFTER A MISSION LASTING NEARLY NINE DAYS.

VALENTINA TERESHKOVA

On June 19, 1963, in the wilds of the Soviet republic of Kazakhstan, herdsmen on horseback found a young Russian woman calmly waiting. Despite her curious appearance—she wore a white helmet and bright orange overalls—the herdsmen hospitably offered bread, cheese, and fermented mare's milk. She was eating heartily when a recovery helicopter arrived. Valentina Tereshkova had just spent almost three days in orbit: the first woman in space. Tereshkova heralded another Soviet new frontier.

LIFE LINES

FULL NAME	VALENTINA VLADIMIROVNA TERESHKOVA
DATE OF BIRTH	MARCH 6, 1937
PLACE OF BIRTH	MASLENNIKOVO, YAROSLAVL, former USSR
EDUCATION	graduated SPINNING TECHNOLOGIST 1961; graduate ZHUKOVSKY AIR FORCE ENGINEERING ACADEMY 1969; CANDIDATE OF TECHNICAL SCIENCES 1976
FAMILY	MARRIED FELLOW COSMONAUT ANDRIAN NIKOLAYEV 1963 (DIVORCED 1982); ONE DAUGHTER, YELENA ANDRIANOVA
CAREER	TEXTILE WORKER 1955–62; JOINED THE COMMUNIST PARTY 1962; COSMONAUT 1963; MEMBER OF OF SUPREME SOVIET 1966; MEMBER OF THE SOVIET CENTRAL COMMITTEE 1974; ELECTED TO CONGRESS OF PEOPLE'S DEPUTIES 1989

STAR WOMAN

Born on March 6, 1937, in the village of Maslennikovo in the Yaroslavl Region, Valentina Tereshkova had a hard childhood. Her father, a tractor driver on a local collective, was killed during World War II. His widow brought up three children on her own. The family moved to the nearby city of Yaroslavl where Valentina had to quit school at the age of sixteen to supplement the family income, first with a job in a tire factory and then, from 1955, as a skilled loom operator in the Krasnyi Perekop Cotton Mill.

She might have spent her life as a factory worker—had it not been for Yuri Gagarin. In 1961 he became the first man in space and inspired thousands of young Soviet citizens to apply for the chance of cosmonaut training. Valentina Tereshkova was one of these citizens.

She never expected to succeed. True, she was fit, strong, and a keen parachutist, but a diploma in cotton-spinning was not exactly a qualification for space. Luckily for her, qualifications mattered little to Soviet leader Nikita Khruschev. He had beaten the Americans by putting the first man in space. Now, he wanted to beat them again.

COSMONAUT CRASH COURSE

The Soviet Vostok capsule did not have to be flown; ground control attended to that. Vostok was really no more than an endurance test, and a woman could endure it at least as well as any man. The only part of the trip that required experience was the parachute descent after reentry. And Valentina Tereshkova had made more than one hundred jumps. Even better, she was also a sound communist.

In February 1962, she was invited to join four other women at the Cosmonaut Training Center. Tereshkova's progress was impressive. Within a year she had a grasp of navigation, geophysics, and spacecraft construction, had passed rigorous physical tests, and could even fly a jet.

She lifted off aboard *Vostok 6* at noon on June 16, 1963, and orbited the Earth forty-eight times in tandem with another capsule, *Vostok 5*, carrying Valeri Bykovsky. The two cosmonauts came within 3 miles (5 km) of each other and regularly beamed TV pictures to the planet below. Tereshkova returned to Earth after two days, 22 hours, and 50 minutes. Bykovsky followed her 2.5 hours later. As Khruschev had intended, her flight stung American pride. Not only was she the first woman in space— she had been out there longer than all the US astronauts put together.

CAREER TIMELINE

March 6, 1937 Born in the Russian village of Maslennikovo.
1953 Leaves school and begins work at a tire factory, but continues to study by correspondence course. Two years later she becomes a loom operator at a cotton mill.
May 21, 1959 Makes first parachute jump at Yaroslavl Aviation Club. Later forms the Textile Mill Workers Parachute Club.
1961 Graduates as a cotton-spinning technologist, becomes secretary of the local Komsomol (Young Communist League).

February 16, 1962 Selected as one of five trainee female cosmonauts (right).
June 16, 1963 Becomes the first woman in space on board *Vostok 6*.
November 3, 1963 Marries fellow cosmonaut Andrian Nikolayev and seven months later, on June 8, 1964, gives birth to a daughter, Yelena Andrianova.
1964 Enters Zhukovsky Military Air Academy to complete her education.

October 1969 Becomes a staff member at the Yuri Gagarin Training School for Cosmonauts. The female cosmonaut detachment is disbanded.
1974 Elected to the Presidium of the Supreme Soviet and becomes a government representative, appearing at numerous international events.
1982 After a prolonged separation she is finally divorced from Andrian Nikolayev.
1989 Elected to Congress of People's Deputies.
1990 After the collapse of communism Tereshkova fades from public life.

> ### I have invaded their little playground.
> VALENTINA TERESHKOVA ON BECOMING A COSMONAUT

After her flight, Tereshkova became an international celebrity. She was given numerous awards including a gold medallion from the British Interplanetary Society in 1964 (above left). Just a few months later, she gave birth to a baby girl (below), an event of some interest to scientists investigating the physiological effects of space travel on women.

After months of training (above left), Valentina Tereshkova became the first woman in space in 1963. Even years after her historic flight, Tereshkova was given VIP treatment. On a visit to England, for example, she became one of the first women to sit at the controls of the supersonic Concorde airliner (top).

NEAR MISS

On January 24, 1969, Tereshkova was nearly killed after a government reception. As the limousines left the Kremlin, an army officer opened fire on the vehicles, hoping to assassinate General Secretary Leonid Brezhnev (below). Tereshkova's car, containing herself and two other cosmonauts, was riddled by bullets. The limousine

NEIL ARMSTRONG

A short hop off the bottom rung of his lunar lander's ladder, and Neil Armstrong was firmly on the Moon's surface—the first human ever to stand upon another world. "That's one small step for man, one giant leap for mankind," Armstrong radioed to Mission Control. The words were his own, not the product of NASA's public relations office. Armstrong messed up his delivery a little—he had meant to say "a man." But the line typified an astronaut who said less so that he could think more.

LIFE LINES

Full Name	Neil Alden Armstrong
Date of Birth	August 5, 1930
Place of Birth	Anglaize County, Ohio
Education	Student at Purdue University 1947–8, 1952–5; BS in aeronautical engineering 1955; MS in aerospace engineering, University of Southern California 1970; several honorary doctorates
Family	Marries Janet Shearon; two children
Career	US Navy pilot 1948–52; test pilot for the National Advisory Committee on Aeronautics, later part of NASA 1955–62; NASA astronaut and aeronautics administrator 1962–71; professor of aeronautical engineering, University of Cincinnati 1971–9; currently chairman of AIL Systems
Date of Death	August 25, 2012

LUNAR LANDER

Even among a team of astronauts selected for their courage, fast reactions, and coolness under pressure, the first man to set foot on the Moon stood out. It seemed Neil Armstrong had no sense of fear.

Once, Armstrong and copilot Edwin "Buzz" Aldrin were practicing the Moon landing in the Lunar Module simulator. The lander began to spin out of control. As it hurtled toward the virtual Moon surface, Armstrong never punched the abort button. They crashed.

Aldrin thought Armstrong had frozen. Aware of NASA's fact-tallying mentality, he worried that the "crash" would be a strike against the two of them. Later, Armstrong said his decision was deliberate. He wanted to test the reactions of ground control—and, equally, test himself.

From childhood, Armstrong set high standards for himself and reached them. Like many boys growing up in the 1940s, he built model airplanes. But he tested his in a homemade wind tunnel. Like many teenagers, he got his first learner's permit at sixteen, but his was for an airplane, not the family car.

SUCCESS IN SPACE

Armstrong flew fighter planes in the Korean War, and later the X-15 rocket plane, before NASA selected him for astronaut training in 1962. He was in space less than four years later.

That first mission was a dramatic success. Before Mission Control had even given them the go-ahead, Armstrong and his copilot performed the first-ever space docking. Half an hour later, they managed to stop their now out-of-control capsule from shaking them to pieces.

After the mission, Armstrong rejoined the astronaut duty roster. His name, along with that of Aldrin and Michael Collins, came up next on the list for the Apollo 11 mission—originally scheduled to be the second landing trip, with Armstrong due to be the third man on the Moon. But when NASA realized that the lunar module would not be ready in time, the plans were moved back. Apollo 10 thoroughly rehearsed every part of the complex Moon mission except the landing itself.

Its smooth success cleared the way for Apollo 11. On July 20, 1969, Armstrong fulfilled US President John F. Kennedy's eight-year-old, $26 billion pledge to put a man on the Moon. Modestly, the astronaut insisted that the thousands of Apollo support personnel be credited, too: "It's their success more than ours."

Two years later, Armstrong left NASA to become a professor of aerospace engineering, and in the late 1970s he went into business. Armstrong died on August 25, 2012.

CAREER TIMELINE

1948–52 US NAVY PILOT. FLIES SEVENTY-EIGHT MISSIONS DURING THE KOREAN WAR. EJECTS TO SAFETY WHEN PLANE STRIKES A TRAP WIRE STRETCHED OVER A VALLEY. RECEIVES THREE MEDALS FOR BRAVERY.
1955 RECEIVES BACHELOR'S DEGREE IN AERONAUTICAL ENGINEERING, PURDUE UNIVERSITY.
1955 MADE TEST PILOT, NATIONAL ADVISORY COUNCIL OF AERONAUTICS, EDWARDS AIR FORCE BASE, CALIFORNIA.
1956 MARRIES JANET SHEARON.

MARCH 16, 1966 *GEMINI 8* LAUNCHES. ARMSTRONG MAKES FIRST-EVER DOCKING IN SPACE, STABILIZING THE CRAFT AFTER FAULTY THRUSTER PUTS CAPSULE IN DANGER.
SEPTEMBER 12–15, 1967 SERVES AS BACKUP PILOT FOR *GEMINI 11* (ON EARTH).
1968 BAILS OUT OF LUNAR LANDING TRAINING VEHICLE SECONDS BEFORE IT CRASHES.
JULY 16, 1969 LAUNCH OF APOLLO 11 MISSION, WHICH TAKES ARMSTRONG, MICHAEL COLLINS, AND

BUZZ ALDRIN TO THE MOON.
JULY 20, 1969 BECOMES FIRST PERSON TO WALK ON THE MOON AFTER LANDING LUNAR MODULE WITH ALDRIN.
JULY 24, 1969 APOLLO 11 RETURNS TO EARTH. CREW IS KEPT IN A MOBILE QUARANTINE FACILITY UNTIL TWENTY-ONE DAYS AFTER LUNAR LIFTOFF.
1971–9 PROFESSOR AT UNIVERSITY OF CINCINNATI.
1986 SERVES ON PRESIDENTIAL COMMISSION ON SPACE SHUTTLE *CHALLENGER* ACCIDENT.

It suddenly struck me that that tiny pea, pretty and blue, was the Earth.
NEIL ARMSTRONG

The Saturn 5 rocket blasted Apollo 11 into space on the morning of July 16, 1969 (far left). Four days later, the lunar module *Eagle* (left) carried Neil Armstrong (top left) and Buzz Aldrin down to the Moon's surface, where they planted the American flag (center). The command module *Columbia* returned safely to Earth on July 24 (below).

The Apollo 11 crew were put into quarantine (above) when they returned to Earth. Their ticker-tape parade through New York was the biggest in history (right).

BUZZ ALDRIN

On July 20, 1969, minutes after Neil Armstrong had stepped out on to the lunar surface, Buzz Aldrin became the second human to walk on the Moon. It was the high point of an impressive career. In the preceding years, Aldrin had not only demonstrated his ability as an astronaut, but had also been instrumental in helping the NASA ground crew solve the technical problems involved in sending people to the Moon. He was both intelligent and practical—just what was needed on the Moon.

LIFE LINES

FULL NAME	BUZZ ALDRIN (ORIGINALLY EDWIN EUGENE ALDRIN JR.; CHANGED TO BUZZ IN 1988)
DATE OF BIRTH	JANUARY 20, 1930
PLACE OF BIRTH	MONTCLAIR, NEW JERSEY
EDUCATION	GRADUATED FROM MONTCLAIR HIGH SCHOOL, 1947; WEST POINT MILITARY ACADEMY, 1948–51; MASSACHUSETTS INSTITUTE OF TECHNOLOGY, 1959–63
FAMILY	MARRIED TO LOIS DRIGGS CANON (THIRD WIFE); THREE CHILDREN FROM PREVIOUS MARRIAGE
CAREER	ACTIVE SERVICE IN KOREA, 1951–3; AERIAL GUNNER INSTRUCTOR, NELLIS AIR FORCE BASE, NEVADA, 1953; AIDE TO FACULTY DEAN AT THE AIR FORCE ACADEMY, 1953–6; PILOT IN 36TH FIGHTER DAY WING IN GERMANY, 1956; TRAINEE ASTRONAUT, 1963; COMMANDER OF THE TEST PILOTS SCHOOL, EDWARDS AIR FORCE BASE, 1971–2

WHAT'S THE BUZZ?

Like nearly all his Apollo colleagues, Buzz Aldrin was a fighter pilot before he became an astronaut. He flew sixty-six missions in the Korean War and shot down two MiG-15s. But he was not one of the test pilots—the elite group from which the vast majority of early astronauts were drawn. He chose a more academic route into space. In 1959, instead of going to the Edwards Air Force Test Pilot School as he had previously planned, Aldrin went to the Massachusetts Institute of Technology. His doctoral thesis, titled "Guidance for Manned Orbital Rendezvous" and written in 1963, contributed directly to the Apollo program. Following this, Aldrin applied to NASA, and in October 1963 was taken on as a trainee astronaut.

He waited for three years before his first mission, but on November 11, 1966, he finally entered orbit aboard *Gemini 12*. He and his Commander Jim Lovell were going to put into practice what Aldrin had spent so long studying—a docking in space. Previous Gemini missions had proved it was possible, but it needed to be perfected if NASA was to send men to the Moon.

Lovell was in the pilot's seat as they approached the target, an Agena rocket stage. But then disaster struck. The radar malfunctioned, meaning that the spacecraft's computer was deprived of the vital data it needed to calculate the trajectories. Undaunted, Aldrin made the necessary calculations on the spot. Lovell guided the spacecraft to a successful docking based on Aldrin's figures. Aldrin then took the controls and put all his theorizing into practice to carry out a flawless docking.

The significance [of Apollo 11] was the reaction of the people watching it...It changed lives.
Buzz Aldrin

The most important week in Aldrin's life began on July 16, 1969, as he prepared for the Moon (far right). The historic event itself (above left) was followed by three weeks in quarantine, which included a meeting with President Nixon (bottom right). Then the crew got a hero's welcome around the world (New York ticker-tape parade, top right).

A LONG JOURNEY HOME

After *Gemini 12*, Aldrin's next spaceflight was to make him the second human on the Moon. With Neil Armstrong he spent over two hours walking on the lunar surface, collecting rocks, and performing simple experiments. It was an incredible achievement, but for Aldrin, the hardest part was coming home. He, Armstrong, and Command Module pilot Michael Collins went on a goodwill world tour on their return. But it wasn't long before life returned to normal, and Aldrin soon suffered a bout of depression. After walking on the Moon, he found it difficult to adjust to an ordinary existence.

Aldrin worked for a time as commander of the Test Pilot School at Edwards Air Force Base before retiring from the Air Force in 1972. He wrote several books, including a frank autobiography that detailed his experience with depression following his time in space. Today, though, he has managed to put his life in order. He travels the world to lecture and promote his own vision of the future of space exploration. In doing so, Aldrin continues to inspire new generations of space travelers—even those too young to remember the Moon landings.

CAREER TIMELINE

1951 Graduates with a Bachelor of Science degree from the West Point Military Academy, New York. Assigned to 51st Fighter Wing in Korea flying F-86s.
1953 Posted to Nellis Air Force Base, Nevada, as an aerial gunner instructor; becomes aide to a faculty dean at the U.S.A.F. Academy, Colorado Springs, Colorado.
1956 F-100 pilot based at Bitburg, Germany.
1959 Goes to Massachusetts Institute of Technology (MIT) to study astronautics.
1963 Gains his doctorate with a thesis called Guidance for Manned Orbital Rendezvous.
October 1963 Joins NASA astronaut team.

August 1965 Capcom (speaking to the astronauts from Mission Control) for *Gemini 5*.
July 1966 Capcom for *Gemini 10*.
November 11, 1966 Launched into space with astronaut Jim Lovell aboard *Gemini 12*.
November 15, 1966 Splashes down in *Gemini 12*.
July 16, 1969 Lifts off aboard Apollo 11 with Neil Armstrong and Michael Collins.
July 20, 1969 Becomes the second man to walk on the Moon (right).
July 24, 1969 Returns to Earth aboard Apollo 11 Command Module.
1971 Becomes Commander of the Test Pilots School at Edwards Air Force Base, California.

1972 Retires from the Air Force and goes into business.
1973 Writes his autobiography, *Return to Earth*.
1989 Writes *Men From Earth*, describing his Apollo mission and his vision of America's future in space, with Malcolm McConell.
1996 *Encounter With Tiber*, a science fiction novel written with John Barnes, is published.

ROCKETS AND LAUNCHERS

The first practical payload-carrying rockets were the A4 or V-2 rockets designed by Wernher von Braun and used by Nazi Germany in 1945. After World War II, V-2s and German scientists fell into Allied hands and V-2 production continued in the US and USSR, where the rockets were used for upper atmosphere science as well as military missile research. Intermediate-range missiles such as the US Redstone followed, and these proved adaptable to carrying manned capsules such as Mercury. Using converted missiles for manned flight purposes was a calculated risk, as they had a worrying tendency to blow up upon launch. Fortunately this never occurred with astronauts aboard. The USSR's first rockets were hardly more successful, particularly the modified SS-6 "Sapwood" missiles lifting early Sputnik and Venera missions, many of which failed to reach orbit. By the mid-1960s purpose-built civilian space launchers such as the Saturn series were replacing military designs, and were followed by the Titan, Delta, and Europe's Ariane series. In addition to the US, Russia, and Europe, India, China, and Japan have flown rockets of their own designs and are likely to be joined by further nations, particularly in Asia.

SATURN SERIES

The 364-foot-tall (111-meter-tall) monster that carried men to the Moon was the last and largest variant of an entire family of Saturn designs. German rocket designer Wernher von Braun and his team of engineers configured their Saturn launcher in a variety of different ways, to serve all of America's potential needs in space. In the end, only three members of the Saturn series ever exchanged the drawing board for the launchpad—the Saturn 1, the upgraded and crew-rated Saturn 1B, and the Moon-bound Saturn 5.

THE SATURN STORY

DECEMBER 30, 1957	WERNHER VON BRAUN PRODUCES A "PROPOSAL FOR A NATIONAL INTEGRATED MISSILE AND SPACE VEHICLE DEVELOPMENT PLAN," WHICH PROPOSES DEVELOPMENT OF THE SATURN 1
JULY 29, 1958	SATURN 1 PROJECT CONTRACT ISSUED BY ARPA
NOVEMBER 2, 1959	TRANSFER OF SATURN 1 PROJECT FROM THE US ARMY TO NASA ANNOUNCED
OCTOBER 27, 1961	FIRST SATURN 1 FLIGHT
JANUARY 5, 1962	NASA ANNOUNCES DEVELOPMENT OF THE SATURN 5 LAUNCH VEHICLE FOR APOLLO
OCTOBER 30, 1963	MANNED SATURN 1 FLIGHTS CANCELED, TO BE REPLACED BY SATURN 1B FLIGHTS
FEBRUARY 26, 1966	FIRST SATURN 1B FLIGHT
NOVEMBER 9, 1967	FIRST SATURN 5 FLIGHT (APOLLO 4)
OCTOBER 11, 1968	FIRST MANNED SATURN 1B FLIGHT (APOLLO 7)
DECEMBER 21, 1968	FIRST MANNED SATURN 5 FLIGHT (APOLLO 8)
JULY 16, 1969	SATURN 5 LIFTS OFF WITH CREW OF APOLLO 11
MAY 14, 1973	FINAL SATURN 5 LAUNCH CARRIES SKYLAB INTO ORBIT IN PLACE OF ITS THIRD STAGE

GROWING FAMILY

The Saturn launchers were the first rockets designed solely to transport men into space. Earlier designs, such as the Redstone, the Atlas, and the Russian R-7, were ballistic missiles modified to carry crew capsules in place of warheads. The Saturns' peaceful origin is perhaps surprising, given that when designer Wernher von Braun and his team began work on the rockets in 1958, they were still employed by the military.

After the US Army plucked the rocket builders out of defeated Nazi Germany in 1945, they worked at the Army Ballistic Missile Agency (ABMA), based in Huntsville, Alabama. But von Braun had always dreamed of the peaceful exploration of space. He proposed a 1.5-million-pound thrust (66,700 kN) booster, ten times more powerful than the existing Jupiter, to be used for the purpose of space exploration. In the aftermath of Russia's surprise launch of *Sputnik 1*, the Pentagon responded very positively to von Braun's proposal. The ABMA began work on a first-stage Saturn booster while also studying possible upper-stage designs.

CLUSTERS, QUICK!

To save time and money, the kerosene and liquid oxygen first stage was built by clustering together eight Rocketdyne H-1 engines—previously used one at a time in the Thor and Jupiter missiles. This raised concerns about whether so many boosters could work together reliably: skeptics dubbed the *Saturn 1* "Cluster's Last Stand." In response, the infant civilian space agency NASA contracted Rocketdyne to build a new engine—the F-1—with enough thrust to match all eight H-1s.

PRESSED FOR TIME

In November 1959, NASA inherited the Saturn program, along with the ABMA itself, from the Army. During the next eighteen months, combination tests of H-1 engines showed cluster fears to be misplaced, and work proceeded on a liquid hydrogen and oxygen upper stage for the Saturn.

The first two-stage Saturn 1 flew from Cape Canaveral on a suborbital test flight on October 27, 1961. Initially, von Braun believed that it would be sufficient to achieve his dream of men on the Moon—the plan was to launch up to fifteen Saturn 1s,

to assemble a moonship in Earth orbit. But President Kennedy's pledge to place a man on the Moon by the end of the decade put a strict deadline on the project that the Saturn 1 plan was simply unable to meet.

To reach the Moon in a single launch, a much more powerful multi-stage rocket would be needed. Von Braun's answer was the three-stage Saturn 5, so-called because it had no less than five mighty F-1 engines clustered together to form the first stage.

As work proceeded on the Saturn 5, the Saturn 1 was upgraded with improved first-stage engines, increased automation with a computerized Instrumentation Unit, and a liquid hydrogen and oxygen upper stage that also served as the third stage for Saturn 5.

This upgraded model, known as

the Saturn 1B, had double the payload capacity of its predecessor, enabling it to be used for flight tests of Apollo hardware. The first uncrewed Saturn 1B flew in February 1966.

The first Saturn 5 followed in November 1967. Just under a year later, a crewed Saturn 1B successfully flew as Apollo 7, followed in December by a crewed Saturn 5 that sent Apollo 8 around the Moon.

For the next four years, Saturn 5s carried men to the lunar surface, and in 1973 the final Saturn 5 hoisted the Skylab space station into low Earth orbit. Meanwhile, Saturn 1Bs carried three separate crews up to Skylab and, in 1975, lifted the Apollo Command Module that docked with a Russian Soyuz spacecraft in orbit. It was a perfect flight record.

WAR AND PEACE

THE SATURN LAUNCHERS WERE DIRECT DESCENDANTS OF THE V2 "VENGEANCE WEAPON" ROCKET (RIGHT) UNLEASHED BY THE NAZIS DURING WORLD WAR II. THE SAME TEAM OF GERMAN ENGINEERS WORKED ON BOTH PROJECTS. SATURN 5 PROGRAM MANAGER ARTHUR RUDOLPH LATER FLED THE US BECAUSE HE WAS BEING INVESTIGATED AS A SUSPECTED WAR CRIMINAL BY FEDERAL AUTHORITIES.

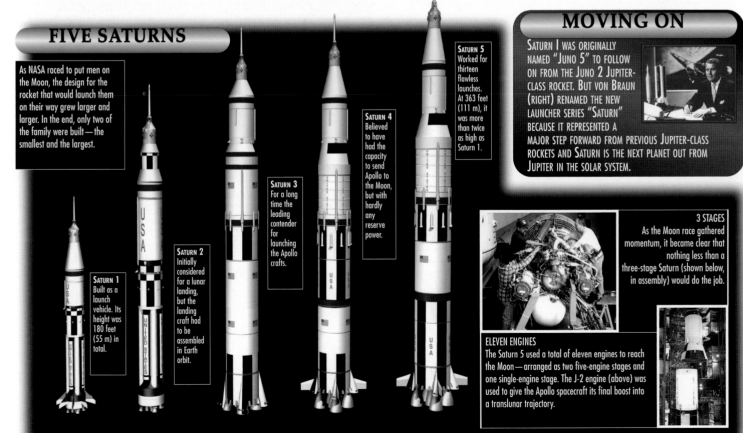

FIVE SATURNS

As NASA raced to put men on the Moon, the design for the rocket that would launch them on their way grew larger and larger. In the end, only two of the family were built—the smallest and the largest.

SATURN 1 Built as a launch vehicle. Its height was 180 feet (55 m) in total.

SATURN 2 Initially considered for a lunar landing, but the landing craft had to be assembled in Earth orbit.

SATURN 3 For a long time the leading contender for launching the Apollo crafts.

SATURN 4 Believed to have had the capacity to send Apollo to the Moon, but with hardly any reserve power.

SATURN 5 Worked for thirteen flawless launches. At 363 feet (111 m), it was more than twice as high as Saturn 1.

MOVING ON

SATURN 1 WAS ORIGINALLY NAMED "JUNO 5" TO FOLLOW ON FROM THE JUNO 2 JUPITER-CLASS ROCKET. BUT VON BRAUN (RIGHT) RENAMED THE NEW LAUNCHER SERIES "SATURN" BECAUSE IT REPRESENTED A MAJOR STEP FORWARD FROM PREVIOUS JUPITER-CLASS ROCKETS AND SATURN IS THE NEXT PLANET OUT FROM JUPITER IN THE SOLAR SYSTEM.

3 STAGES
As the Moon race gathered momentum, it became clear that nothing less than a three-stage Saturn (shown below, in assembly) would do the job.

ELEVEN ENGINES
The Saturn 5 used a total of eleven engines to reach the Moon—arranged as two five-engine stages and one single-engine stage. The J-2 engine (above) was used to give the Apollo spacecraft its final boost into a translunar trajectory.

SOYUZ SERIES

T he orbiting workhorse of the Soviet and Russian space programs was first proposed in 1962 as a two-man capsule for space rendezvous and docking that could also be used on a Moon mission. But as with the disaster that killed three Apollo astronauts in January 1967, catastrophe forced the redesign of the craft. The Soyuz ("Union") capsule that emerged proved phenomenally successful, flying more than one hundred missions. In modified form, it will be used well into this century—over forty years after its first flight.

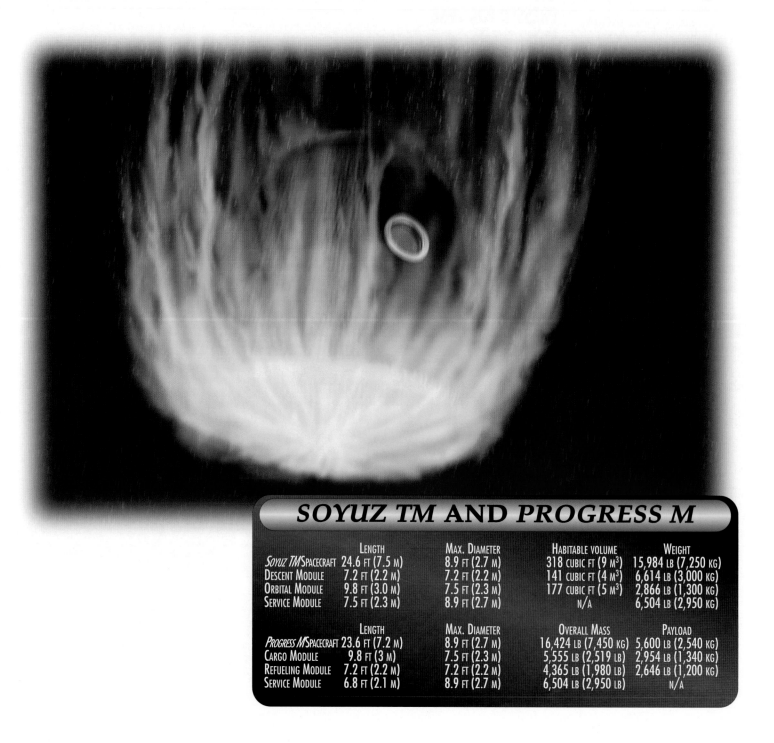

SOYUZ TM AND PROGRESS M

	LENGTH	MAX. DIAMETER	HABITABLE VOLUME	WEIGHT
Soyuz TM Spacecraft	24.6 FT (7.5 M)	8.9 FT (2.7 M)	318 CUBIC FT (9 M³)	15,984 LB (7,250 KG)
DESCENT MODULE	7.2 FT (2.2 M)	7.2 FT (2.2 M)	141 CUBIC FT (4 M³)	6,614 LB (3,000 KG)
ORBITAL MODULE	9.8 FT (3.0 M)	7.5 FT (2.3 M)	177 CUBIC FT (5 M³)	2,866 LB (1,300 KG)
SERVICE MODULE	7.5 FT (2.3 M)	8.9 FT (2.7 M)	N/A	6,504 LB (2,950 KG)

	LENGTH	MAX. DIAMETER	OVERALL MASS	PAYLOAD
Progress M Spacecraft	23.6 FT (7.2 M)	8.9 FT (2.7 M)	16,424 LB (7,450 KG)	5,600 LB (2,540 KG)
CARGO MODULE	9.8 FT (3 M)	7.5 FT (2.3 M)	5,555 LB (2,519 LB)	2,954 LB (1,340 KG)
REFUELING MODULE	7.2 FT (2.2 M)	7.2 FT (2.2 M)	4,365 LB (1,980 LB)	2,646 LB (1,200 KG)
SERVICE MODULE	6.8 FT (2.1 M)	8.9 FT (2.7 M)	6,504 LB (2,950 LB)	N/A

SPACE CARRIER

Soyuz is the most successful series of spacecraft yet built, but its early days were dogged by disaster. The first Soyuz flight, in April 1967, ended in tragedy. Its pilot, Vladimir Komarov, was killed when the craft crashed after reentry. It took eighteen months for the program to recover, with a successful orbital near-docking of *Soyuz 2* and *Soyuz 3*.

Then in June 1971, another catastrophe struck. Three cosmonauts were sent aloft in *Soyuz 11* and transferred to a new 20-ton (18.1 t) space station, Salyut. This new Soviet "first" drew tremendous publicity, but when *Soyuz 11* returned to Earth, on June 30, its occupants were found dead in their capsule. A valve had been jolted open during reentry, releasing all the capsule's air, and the crew had suffocated.

But the Soviets continued developing Soyuz and produced a thoroughly reliable design. Their faith in the craft was publicly demonstrated in 1975, when a Soyuz docked successfully in orbit with a US Apollo spacecraft. This Apollo-Soyuz linkup led nowhere, because the Apollo program was almost over. But Soyuz soldiered on. After thirty-four missions, it was updated to the T (for "transport") version and ferried crews to and from the Salyut space stations. These space station missions were supported with supplies sent up in Soyuz's uncrewed version, Progress. And in a third incarnation, the TM series, some two dozen Soyuz missions enabled cosmonauts to build the first giant space station, Mir.

SOYUZ TM

The latest crew-carrying version of Soyuz, the *TM*, is a three-part vehicle consisting of a descent module, an orbital module, and a service module. The bell-shaped descent module, about 7 feet (2.1 m) long and 7 feet (2.1 m) in diameter, is where the crew of three stays during launch, orbital maneuvers, and reentry, and contains the spacecraft's main control systems. It sits between the orbital and service modules, and is the only part of the spacecraft that returns to Earth at the end of a mission—the orbital and service modules are jettisoned during reentry and are left to burn up in the atmosphere. The descent module carries the cosmonauts back through the atmosphere, using parachutes to slow descent and retrorockets to ensure a safe and soft landing for the crew.

The near-spherical orbital module, positioned in front of the descent module, carries life-support and rendezvous and docking systems. Its habitable internal volume is about 177 cubic feet (5 m³)—about 25 percent more than that of the descent module. When Soyuz is coasting in orbit, the module serves as the cosmonauts' working, recreation, and sleeping quarters, and when the craft is docked to the Mir space station or the International Space Station, it functions as an air lock.

The service module, to the rear of the descent module, is over 7 feet (2.1 m) long with a diameter of nearly 9 feet (2.7 m). It contains the orbital flight systems, including propulsion and maneuvering engines, and a pair of winglike solar panels with a span of about 35 feet (10.6 m).

The panels are stowed away during the mission's launch phase and unfurl when the craft is in orbit. They have a total area of about 108 square feet (10 m²) and generate 600 watts of electricity for the craft, which also carries batteries.

HARD EVIDENCE

SOFT LANDING
When Yuri Gagarin returned to Earth after making the first human spaceflight, he ejected from his Vostok capsule after reentry and parachuted to the ground. With Soyuz, which holds two or three cosmonauts, ejection is impossible, so it descends by parachute (left). Just before landing, rocket engines cut in to slow its fall, allowing it to land gently at a mere 2 mph (3.2 kmh). On several occasions these rockets have failed, making touchdown bumpy but survivable.

SOYUZ SPACECRAFT

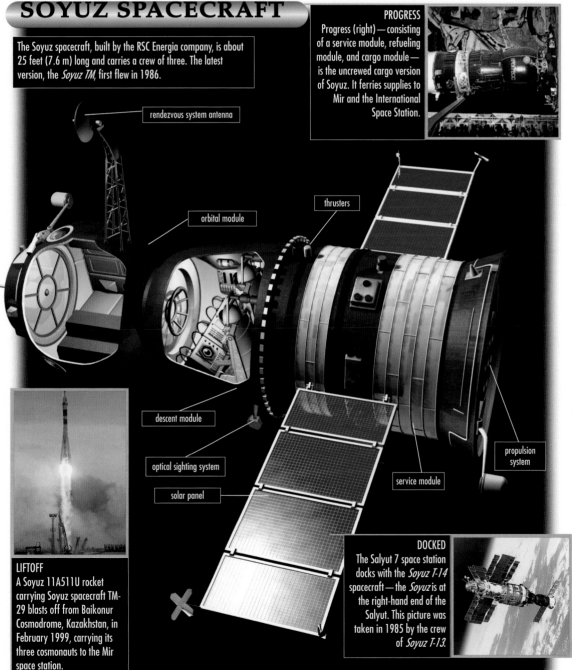

The Soyuz spacecraft, built by the RSC Energia company, is about 25 feet (7.6 m) long and carries a crew of three. The latest version, the *Soyuz TM*, first flew in 1986.

PROGRESS
Progress (right)—consisting of a service module, refueling module, and cargo module—is the uncrewed cargo version of Soyuz. It ferries supplies to Mir and the International Space Station.

rendezvous system antenna

orbital module

thrusters

descent module

optical sighting system

solar panel

service module

propulsion system

LIFTOFF
A Soyuz 11A511U rocket carrying Soyuz spacecraft TM-29 blasts off from Baikonur Cosmodrome, Kazakhstan, in February 1999, carrying its three cosmonauts to the Mir space station.

DOCKED
The Salyut 7 space station docks with the *Soyuz T-14* spacecraft—the *Soyuz* is at the right-hand end of the Salyut. This picture was taken in 1985 by the crew of *Soyuz T-13*.

SHUTTLES AND STATIONS

Mankind has long dreamed of a permanent habitation in space. Science fiction writers, artists, and filmmakers depicted massive stations serving as communities or staging posts for missions to the stars. The massive wheel-like space stations of sci-fi publications and films such as *2001: A Space Odyssey* have not yet come to pass. The Soviet Soyuz and US Skylab were followed by the long-lived Mir, but all eventually fell to Earth when their working lives were over, and today the International Space Station (ISS) is the only permanently manned outpost in space. Of course, a space station needs a means of delivering and returning its residents and their provisions, as well as getting its components into orbit in the first place. Constructing and servicing a station was one rationale behind the Space Transportation System or Space Shuttle, first proposed at the end of the Apollo program. Critics of NASA say that the Space Shuttle's only justification was to support the ISS, and the ISS only exists to give the Shuttle a mission, although since its retirement in 2011, commercial launches have been used to supply the ISS. While there is still some urgency to the development of the new Crew Exploration Vehicle, there has now been a gap of several years during which the US has not had its own manned launch capability.

SALYUTS 1–5

The early Soviet space stations, launched in the 1970s, went from problems to solutions and tragedy to triumph. What started as a hasty modification of the Almaz military space station—to regain Soviet prestige after the Americans beat them to the Moon—developed into a world-leading mastery of space technology. During the Salyut program, ingenious designers had to struggle with unreliable launch systems and changing priorities, while brave cosmonauts faced the constant threat of death.

MISSIONS TO SALYUTS

Mission	Date	Result
Soyuz 10	April 1971	Failure. Unable to dock properly
Soyuz 11	June 1971	Failure. Crew killed on reentry
Soyuz 14	July 1974	Success. Military mission to Salyut 3
Soyuz 15	August 1974	Failure. Nearly rams Salyut 3
Soyuz 17	January 1975	Success. First mission to Salyut 4
Soyuz 18–1	April 1975	Failure. suborbital launch abort
Soyuz 18	May 1975	Success. Crew spends two months on Salyut 4
Soyuz 21	July 1976	Partial success. Crew makes emergency return from Salyut 5
Soyuz 23	October 1976	Failure. Docking fails: splashdown return
Soyuz 24	February 1977	Success. End of operations on Salyut 5

SPACE OUTPOSTS

In 1969, the Soviets lost the race to the Moon. But they had a functional spacecraft—the Soyuz moonship—and space-station hulls built for the Almaz military program. By combining these two technologies, they could build a space station and beat the Americans that way.

Salyut 1 was an Almaz with Soyuz systems bolted on. Two small sets of solar panels were fitted to provide electrical power, and a Soyuz service module was placed at the rear. The front docking port replaced the Almaz's return capsule and its self-defense gun (a Nudelman 23mm cannon). Then came two examples of the "standard" military Almaz, Salyuts 2 and 3. Salyut 4 was civilian, with improved systems, but Salyut 5 was another Almaz.

With each new Salyut, increasingly advanced technology was tested. Salyuts 3 and 5 were fitted with gyroscopes that controlled the stations' orientation. Similar systems have since been used for Mir and the International Space Station (ISS). Salyut 4 incorporated a computer that automatically kept the station pointed in the correct direction. And in November 1975, *Soyuz 20* and Salyut 4 achieved the world's first uncrewed docking, proving the technology used by Progress ferries and the later Soviet stations.

SCIENCE ON SALYUT

The military origins of Salyut meant that much of the main compartment was taken up by a housing for a spy camera or telescope. Although Moscow was keen to publicize the economic advantages of photographing the

RED STARS IN ORBIT

Soyuz 17

SALYUT 4

SALYUT 3

SPACE HOTHOUSE
Cosmonauts Pyotr Klimuk and Vitaly Sevastyanov demonstrate the equipment necessary for growing plants aboard Salyut 4 in 1975.

INSIDE STORY
The interior of the world's first successful space station, Salyut 1. This station was launched in April 1971, where it remained in orbit for 175 days.

Salyut 4, seen here docking with the *Soyuz 17* ferry craft, went into service while Salyut 3 was still in orbit. Salyut 3, a military space station probably on a reconnaissance mission, flew in a lower orbit than the civilian Salyut 4. It reentered the atmosphere and burned up on January 24, 1975, nearly a month after Salyut 4 was launched.

Earth, much of the Salyuts' photographic activity was a cover for military missions to evaluate the potential of crewed spy satellites. But some observations were very important: Salyuts 4 and 5 used an infrared spectrometer to measure the water content of the stratosphere, and were therefore able to discover some of the first signs of ozone depletion.

Biology was covered by Salyuts 1 and 4, which had miniature greenhouses where cosmonauts tried to grow plants. These stations also carried out many astronomical observations, mainly in wavelengths blocked by the atmosphere. Salyut 1's primary instrument was an ultraviolet telescope, while Salyut 4's was a solar telescope. The instrument was crippled by a broken sensor, but the *Soyuz 17* crew learned to steer it by controlling its servomotors by ear.

During the operational lives of the first Salyut stations, great progress was also made in the medical evaluation and consequences of long-duration flights: by 1977, thirteen cosmonauts had each flown in space for more than two weeks at a time.

MISSION DIARY: SALYUTS 1–5

APRIL 19, 1971 SALYUT 1 IS LAUNCHED FROM BAIKONUR COSMODROME ON A PROTON ROCKET.
APRIL 23, 1971 THE *SOYUZ 10* SPACECRAFT TAKES OFF CARRYING THE FIRST CREW (RIGHT) TO VISIT SALYUT 1. THE CREWS ARE UNABLE TO DOCK SUCCESSFULLY WITH THE SPACE STATION AND RETURN TO EARTH ON APRIL 25.
JUNE 7, 1971 THE CREW OF *SOYUZ 11*—GEORGY DOBROVOLSKY, VIKTOR PATSAYEV, AND VLADISLAV VOLKOV—(ABOVE) SUCCESSFULLY DOCK WITH SALYUT 1 AND STAY UNTIL JUNE 29. THE MISSION ENDS IN TRAGEDY WHEN ALL THREE DIE AFTER THEIR CAPSULE CABIN PRESSURE

FAILS AT REENTRY.
JULY 29, 1972 A SOVIET ATTEMPT TO PUT ANOTHER SPACE STATION INTO ORBIT FAILS WHEN IT IS DESTROYED DURING THE LAUNCH.
APRIL 3, 1973 SALYUT 2 IS LAUNCHED SUCCESSFULLY FROM BAIKONUR, BUT IT BREAKS UP IN ORBIT.
MAY 11, 1973 ANOTHER SALYUT, CODENAMED COSMOS 557, IS LAUNCHED BUT GOES OUT OF CONTROL AND REENTERS THE ATMOSPHERE ON MAY 22.
JUNE 25, 1974 SALYUT 3, A MILITARY SPACE STATION, IS LAUNCHED FROM BAIKONUR.
JULY 3, 1974 *SOYUZ 14* IS LAUNCHED, CARRYING COSMONAUTS PAVEL POPOVICH AND YURI ARTYUKHIN TO SALYUT 3. THEY STAY ABOARD THE STATION UNTIL JULY 19.

DECEMBER 26, 1974 SALYUT 4 IS LAUNCHED.
JANUARY 11, 1975 ALEXEI GUBAREV AND GEORGY GRECHKO (RIGHT) TAKE OFF ON *SOYUZ 17* FOR A FOUR-WEEK VISIT TO SALYUT 4.
JUNE 22, 1976 SALYUT 5, A MILITARY SPACE STATION, IS LAUNCHED SUCCESSFULLY FROM BAIKONUR.
JULY 6, 1976 *SOYUZ 21* CARRIES BORIS VOLYNOV AND VITALY ZHOLOBOV TO SALYUT 5.
FEBRUARY 7, 1976 YURI GLAZKOV AND VIKTOR GORBATKO LIFT OFF ON *SOYUZ 24*, THE FINAL MISSION TO SALYUT 5.

SALYUTS
6 AND 7

T he operation of the two space stations Salyuts 6 and 7 from 1977 to 1986 was a vital stage in the development of human spaceflight. The experience gained was crucial to later successful operations on the Mir space station and for future human missions into the solar system. Cosmonauts worked routinely aboard the stations, carrying out a wide range of experiments as well as acting as orbiting repairmen. Salyuts 6 and 7 clearly placed the Soviet Union ahead of the rest in the field of long-duration spaceflight.

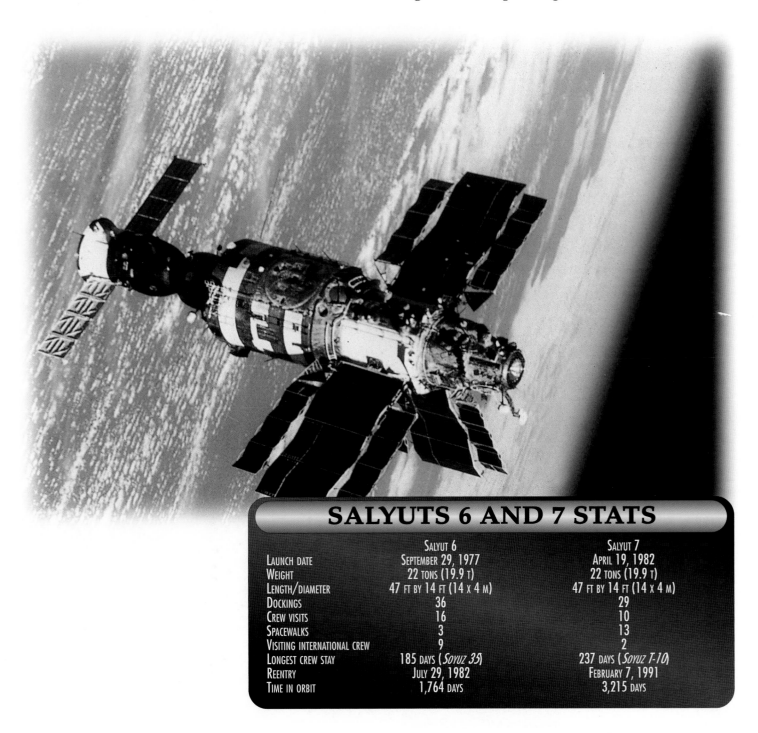

SALYUTS 6 AND 7 STATS

	Salyut 6	Salyut 7
Launch date	September 29, 1977	April 19, 1982
Weight	22 tons (19.9 t)	22 tons (19.9 t)
Length/diameter	47 ft by 14 ft (14 x 4 m)	47 ft by 14 ft (14 x 4 m)
Dockings	36	29
Crew visits	16	10
Spacewalks	3	13
Visiting international crew	9	2
Longest crew stay	185 days (Soyuz 35)	237 days (Soyuz T-10)
Reentry	July 29, 1982	February 7, 1991
Time in orbit	1,764 days	3,215 days

THE LONG RUN

When Salyut 6 reached orbit in September 1977, it marked an important step toward the construction of a permanent orbiting space station. The improved Salyut station had two docking ports and could receive two spacecraft at once. This meant that refueling of the propulsion engine and crew changes could both take place in orbit.

Salyut 6 was planned to support long-duration missions of between 90 and 180 days. But the Soyuz ferry spacecraft were only designed to stay in space for about 80 days. So the main crew would spend a long mission on the space station and other crews would arrive in a new Soyuz and depart in the main crew's Soyuz. These secondary crews would often include a guest cosmonaut from socialist countries such as Czechoslovakia, Cuba, Vietnam, East Germany, Mongolia, and Poland.

Salyut 6 marked the first use of the uncrewed Progress cargo ferries. These brought supplies for the crew as well as fuel for the station. Progress was also used as a space tug to boost the station's orbit. Before releasing the cargo ship to burn up in the atmosphere the crews would stuff all their refuse, dirty clothes, and redundant equipment into the ferry.

Over a period of four years, five long-stay crews visited the outpost, notching up mission durations of 96, 140, 175, 185, and 75 days. In addition, eleven short-stay crews visited. The crews carried out hundreds of experiments and occupied Salyut 6 for 676 days, far ahead of the 171 days' occupation of the US Skylab station.

RECORD BREAKER

Salyut 7 entered orbit with several improvements, including larger and stronger docking ports, an improved computer, a refrigerator, and even hot and cold running water. The first crew aboard Salyut 7 set a new world record by spending 211 days in orbit, and the third long-stay crew managed an even longer stay of 237 days.

Salyut 7 suffered many technical breakdowns during its life and its crews had to repeatedly carry out repairs both inside and outside the station. During its time in orbit, two large modules docked with Salyut 7, bringing supplies and providing a larger work area for the crew. These modules were the forerunners of the type later used on the Mir station.

Salyut 7 crews had their fair share of frightening moments. During the *Soyuz T-9* flight, the crew began to evacuate the station when they heard a loud crack. On investigation they discovered that a micrometeorite or piece of space debris had hit one of the station's windows leaving a tiny crater.

Although not quite as successful as Salyut 6, Salyut 7 met its objectives—and in the process established the Soviet Union as the then undisputed leader in long-duration crewed spaceflight.

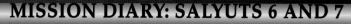

MISSION DIARY: SALYUTS 6 AND 7

SEPTEMBER 29, 1977 SALYUT 6 IS LAUNCHED FROM BAIKONUR COSMODROME.
OCTOBER 9, 1977 THE FIRST CREW TO VISIT SALYUT 6, VALERY RYUMIN AND VLADIMIR KOVALENOK (ABOVE, LEFT TO RIGHT), FAIL TO DOCK WITH THE STATION.
JANUARY 23–4, 1978 SALYUT 6 IS REFUELED FOR THE FIRST TIME FROM THE DOCKED *PROGRESS 1* CARGO SPACECRAFT.
MARCH 2, 1978 *SOYUZ 28* FERRIES THE FIRST INTERNATIONAL CREW TO SALYUT 6.
APRIL 9, 1980 COSMONAUTS LEONID POPOV AND VALERY RYUMIN ARE LAUNCHED ABOARD *SOYUZ 35*. THEY SPEND A RECORD 185 DAYS IN ORBIT.
MARCH 1981 VICTOR SAVINYKH BECOMES THE ONE HUNDREDTH TRAVELER IN SPACE ON A MISSION TO SALYUT 6.

APRIL 19, 1982 SALYUT 7 (BELOW LEFT, BEING ASSEMBLED) IS LAUNCHED.
MAY 13–DECEMBER 10, 1982 SALYUT 7'S FIRST CREW SPEND 211 DAYS ABOARD THE SPACE STATION.
JUNE 24, 1982 FRENCH "SPATIONAUTE" JEAN-LOUP CHRÉTIEN SPENDS A WEEK ABOARD SALYUT 7.
FEBRUARY 1985 MISSION CONTROLLERS LOSE CONTACT WITH SALYUT 7.
JUNE 1985 THE *SOYUZ T-13* CREW BRINGS THE TUMBLING, FROZEN SALYUT 7 BACK TO LIFE (ABOVE).
MAY 6, 1986 *SOYUZ T-15* CREW FLY FROM MIR TO SALYUT 7 TO COMPLETE EXPERIMENTS BEGUN BY THE *SOYUZ T-14* CREW.
FEBRUARY 7, 1991 SALYUT 7 REENTERS EARTH'S ATMOSPHERE OVER SOUTH AMERICA.

SALYUT 7 IN ORBIT

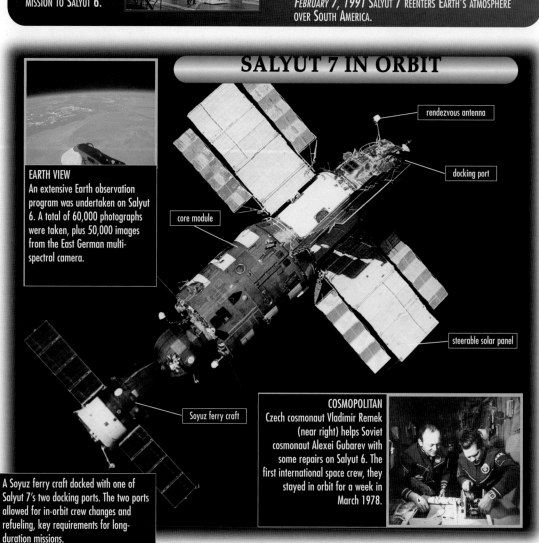

EARTH VIEW
An extensive Earth observation program was undertaken on Salyut 6. A total of 60,000 photographs were taken, plus 50,000 images from the East German multi-spectral camera.

rendezvous antenna

docking port

core module

steerable solar panel

Soyuz ferry craft

A Soyuz ferry craft docked with one of Salyut 7's two docking ports. The two ports allowed for in-orbit crew changes and refueling, key requirements for long-duration missions.

COSMOPOLITAN
Czech cosmonaut Vladimir Remek (near right) helps Soviet cosmonaut Alexei Gubarev with some repairs on Salyut 6. The first international space crew, they stayed in orbit for a week in March 1978.

SOYUZ 11 DISASTER

I n the early hours of June 30, 1971, recovery crews were gathered near the Soviet space complex at Baikonur, on the prairie-like steppes of Kazakhstan, to await the landing of the *Soyuz 11* spacecraft. Its crew of three—cosmonauts Dobrovolsky, Patsayev, and Volkov—had completed a record-breaking twenty-three days in orbit in the world's first space station, Salyut 1. A heroes' welcome had been prepared, and the ground crew was overjoyed as the craft landed perfectly—but the world soon discovered all was not as it seemed.

THE *SOYUZ 11* CREW

VLADISLAV NIKOLAYEVICH VOLKOV
BORN: NOVEMBER 23, 1935, IN MOSCOW, SOVIET UNION (NOW IN RUSSIA)
PREVIOUS SPACEFLIGHT: *SOYUZ 7*,

1969
GEORGY TIMAFEYEVICH DOBROVOLSKY
BORN: JUNE 1, 1928, IN ODESSA, SOVIET UNION (NOW IN UKRAINE)
PREVIOUS SPACEFLIGHTS: NONE

VIKTOR PATSAYEV
BORN: JUNE 19, 1933, IN AKTYUBINSK, SOVIET UNION (NOW IN KAZAKHSTAN)
PREVIOUS SPACEFLIGHTS: NONE

DESCENT TO DEATH

The modern era of crewed space exploration, which focuses on orbiting space stations, began on June 7, 1971. On that day, Georgy Dobrovolsky, Viktor Patsayev, and Vladislav Volkov squeezed through the docking port of their *Soyuz 11* spacecraft—callsign Yantar ("Amber")—into Salyut 1, the world's first space station. Soviet space scientists, and many others, saw space stations with replaceable crews as the main highway into space. On these orbiting platforms, the craft that would take humanity to explore the solar system and beyond would be built and launched.

The crew's first task was to check all of the systems in the united craft—especially those of Salyut, which had already been in orbit for almost two months. They then settled into a routine of Earth-science observations and medical and biological experiments. They were to have made solar observations, but the large solar telescope was inoperable because its cover had failed to jettison.

They also had exercise equipment—a treadmill and a bungee-string—to help prevent their muscles from wasting away through lack of use. But what looked good on the ground turned out to be unusable in space. Just one 180-pound (82 kg) man throwing himself around proved more than the combined vehicles could take, and the exercises were abandoned.

Then, about three weeks into the mission, the station itself was abandoned. A series of difficulties, and a small electrical fire a week earlier, had persuaded the Soviets of the need to cut the mission short. The crew gathered up their data, transferred back into *Soyuz 11*, and returned to Earth.

FINAL JOURNEY

At 9:28 p.m. on the evening of June 29, Georgy Dobrovolsky undocked the Soyuz craft from Salyut 1. After three orbits of the Earth, Dobrovolsky called Mission Control to tell them that they were beginning their descent. Mission Control radioed back, "Goodbye, Yantar, till we see you soon on Mother Earth." At 1:35 a.m., the craft's retrorockets fired and it began its descent through the atmosphere. Then its parachutes deployed and it floated gently down to the ground.

Although the craft made a near-perfect landing, the cosmonauts

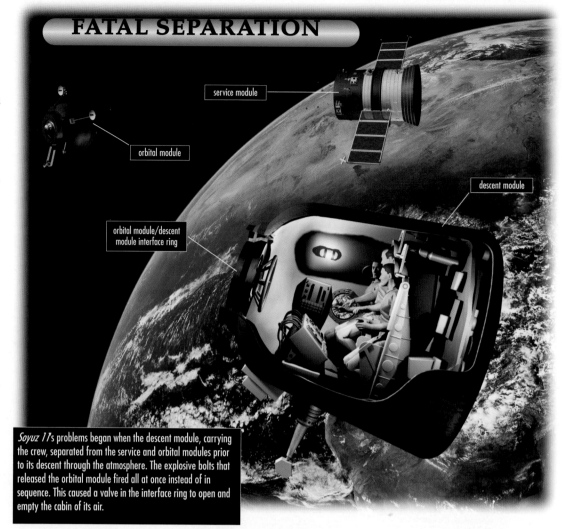

FATAL SEPARATION

service module

orbital module

descent module

orbital module/descent module interface ring

Soyuz 11's problems began when the descent module, carrying the crew, separated from the service and orbital modules prior to its descent through the atmosphere. The explosive bolts that released the orbital module fired all at once instead of in sequence. This caused a valve in the interface ring to open and empty the cabin of its air.

never reached the ground alive. Some 723 seconds after the retrorockets had fired, the twelve explosive bolts that released the descent module from the orbital module fired at once instead of in a controlled sequence. This shook open an air pressure equalization valve, at an altitude of 104 miles (167 km). With appalling speed, the capsule's air hissed into space.

Patsayev unbuckled his safety harness and tried desperately to close or block the valve, but failed. Within about nine or ten seconds, decompression emptied the crew's lungs—none of them were wearing space suits—and they died within about thirty seconds. A mission that should have been a triumph of breakthroughs in Soviet technology had turned into a tragedy.

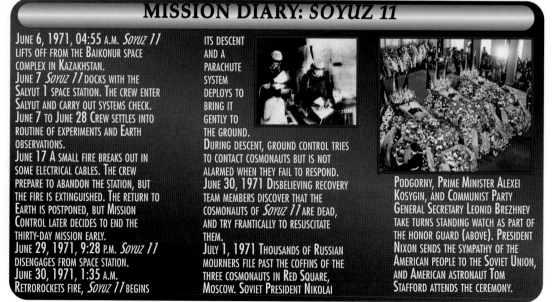

MISSION DIARY: *SOYUZ 11*

JUNE 6, 1971, 04:55 A.M. *SOYUZ 11* LIFTS OFF FROM THE BAIKONUR SPACE COMPLEX IN KAZAKHSTAN.
JUNE 7 *SOYUZ 11* DOCKS WITH THE SALYUT 1 SPACE STATION. THE CREW ENTER SALYUT AND CARRY OUT SYSTEMS CHECK.
JUNE 7 TO JUNE 28 CREW SETTLES INTO ROUTINE OF EXPERIMENTS AND EARTH OBSERVATIONS.
JUNE 17 A SMALL FIRE BREAKS OUT IN SOME ELECTRICAL CABLES. THE CREW PREPARE TO ABANDON THE STATION, BUT THE FIRE IS EXTINGUISHED. THE RETURN TO EARTH IS POSTPONED, BUT MISSION CONTROL LATER DECIDES TO END THE THIRTY-DAY MISSION EARLY.
JUNE 29, 1971, 9:28 P.M. *SOYUZ 11* DISENGAGES FROM SPACE STATION.
JUNE 30, 1971, 1:35 A.M. RETROROCKETS FIRE, *SOYUZ 11* BEGINS

ITS DESCENT AND A PARACHUTE SYSTEM DEPLOYS TO BRING IT GENTLY TO THE GROUND.
DURING DESCENT, GROUND CONTROL TRIES TO CONTACT COSMONAUTS BUT IS NOT ALARMED WHEN THEY FAIL TO RESPOND.
JUNE 30, 1971 DISBELIEVING RECOVERY TEAM MEMBERS DISCOVER THAT THE COSMONAUTS OF *SOYUZ 11* ARE DEAD, AND TRY FRANTICALLY TO RESUSCITATE THEM.
JULY 1, 1971 THOUSANDS OF RUSSIAN MOURNERS FILE PAST THE COFFINS OF THE THREE COSMONAUTS IN RED SQUARE, MOSCOW. SOVIET PRESIDENT NIKOLAI

PODGORNY, PRIME MINISTER ALEXEI KOSYGIN, AND COMMUNIST PARTY GENERAL SECRETARY LEONID BREZHNEV TAKE TURNS STANDING WATCH AS PART OF THE HONOR GUARD (ABOVE). PRESIDENT NIXON SENDS THE SYMPATHY OF THE AMERICAN PEOPLE TO THE SOVIET UNION, AND AMERICAN ASTRONAUT TOM STAFFORD ATTENDS THE CEREMONY.

SKYLAB

The Apollo Applications Program was started in 1966 to conduct extended lunar operations and long-duration crewed missions in orbit around the Earth. Using the vast power of the Saturn 5 rocket, the program planned an ambitious series of space stations in orbit. When budget cuts forced mission planners to scale down their ideas, just one project survived: the Skylab Orbital Workshop. Launched in 1973, Skylab was America's first space station, paving the way for the International Space Station (ISS)—and still holds the record as the world's largest orbiting spacecraft.

SKYLAB SPECS

OVERALL LENGTH (INCLUDING CSM) 118.5 FT (36 M)	ORBITAL WORKSHOP
OVERALL WORKING VOLUME 11,700 CU FT (481 M3)	LENGTH 48.1 FT (14.6 M)
	DIAMETER 21.6 FT (6.6 M)
POWER OUTPUT 4,000 WATTS AT 28 VOLTS DC	WEIGHT (WITH SOLAR PANEL) 167,850 LB (76,135 KG)
	WORKING VOLUME 9,550 CU FT (270 M3)
	AMBIENT TEMPERATURE 70°F (21°C)

BASE IN SPACE

The great advantage of Skylab was that it was already half-built even before it was formally approved as a new project in 1969. The idea had occurred to master rocket designer Wernher von Braun four years earlier. During lunch one day, he casually doodled on a paper napkin how his invention, the Saturn 5 rocket, could be recycled as an Earth-orbiting space station.

Normally, the third stage of the Saturn 5 carried fuel for the Apollo spacecraft's trip out of Earth orbit to the Moon. But if this stage remained in Earth orbit, the propellants and rocket engines for the Moon journey would not be needed, and neither would the fuel to power them. The huge tanks could be filled with air instead, divided into compartments, and made into a giant facility for astronauts to live and work in.

CONVERTED ROCKET

In 1970, when two Apollo Moon landing missions were canceled, the available Saturn 5 was converted into Skylab.

Inside, what was once the hydrogen tank was converted into a two-story space where three astronauts could live and work together. They would breathe a mixture of nitrogen and oxygen, while a thermal and ventilation system provided an ambient temperature of 70°F (21°C). The first story was divided into living areas, with a ward room, sleeping compartments, and a bathroom. Above was the work space, where the crew could "swim" in weightless conditions and carry out experiments. Enough food, water, and clothing was stowed on board for all three missions scheduled to visit Skylab.

Outside, Skylab carried what were then the largest solar panels ever used on a spaceship. On top was the Apollo Telescope Mount (ATM), a solar observatory with an array of instruments including X-ray, infrared, and visible light cameras. ATM allowed the Sun's structure and chemistry to be observed in great detail for the first time. Skylab was launched unmanned on May 14, 1973, on the last-ever Saturn 5 booster to fly. In all, three crews visited it over two years, and the space station provided NASA and these nine astronauts with their first valuable experiences of living and working in orbit for long periods.

After six years and 34,981 orbits, Skylab met its end. Increased sunspot activity had expanded the Earth's atmosphere, and this, together with difficulties in maintaining a low-drag altitude, meant that the space station was drawn inexorably Earthward. On July 11, 1979, Skylab crashed home. Though some large pieces of the space station landed in Western Australia, most of the debris—mainly the craft's "skin"—fell harmlessly into the Indian Ocean.

CLEAN CREW

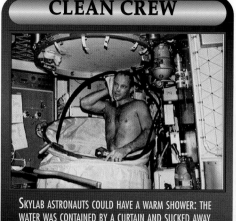

SKYLAB ASTRONAUTS COULD HAVE A WARM SHOWER: THE WATER WAS CONTAINED BY A CURTAIN AND SUCKED AWAY BY A VACUUM SYSTEM. BUT THE CREW COULD NOT WASH THEIR CLOTHES. INSTEAD, THEY WORE DISPOSABLE GARMENTS. THE STATION'S LOCKERS CONTAINED 39 JACKETS AND 69 PANTS, 30 PAIRS OF BOOTS, AND 197 SETS OF UNDERWEAR.

FOOTHOLD
Triangular weights fitted to the undersides of the astronauts' shoes gripped the wire grid floor to prevent the crew from floating away in zero gravity.

FINGERTIP
Skylab 3's crew worked hard at their physical exercises, which were part of the experiments in living in weightlessness and guarded against muscle wastage. Here, Commander Carr jokingly "balances" Pilot Pogue on his head with just one finger.

DOCKED
The Apollo command and service module that carried the three-man crew to Skylab remained attached to Skylab. Sometimes, astronauts would retreat into it for a moment of peace and privacy.

SKYLAB

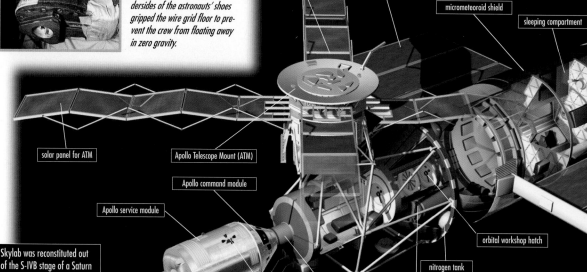

Skylab was reconstituted out of the S-IVB stage of a Saturn 5 rocket. It provided a long-term home away from home for US astronauts and also functioned as a large orbital laboratory.

ATM sensors

solar panel

micrometeoroid shield

sleeping compartment

waste tanks

altitude control nitrogen bottles

solar panel for ATM

Apollo Telescope Mount (ATM)

Apollo command module

Apollo service module

propulsion engine nozzle

vernier control motors

docking hatch

oxygen tank

ATM support struts

nitrogen tank

orbital workshop hatch

solar panel deployment boom

COLUMBIA'S FIRST FLIGHT

Until the launch of the Space Shuttle *Columbia* in 1981, almost all rockets were used only once—an immensely wasteful practice. *Columbia* was designed to take off vertically as a rocket and land horizontally as an airplane. Only the main tank was disposable. The new Space Shuttle's orbiter section, with crew cabin, payload bay, wings, and engines, was built to survive up to one hundred missions over twenty years. Even the solid fuel boosters were reusable. But *Columbia*'s debut flight had some alarming moments.

STS-1 STATISTICS

CRAFT   *COLUMBIA*
MISSION STS-1 (SPACE TRANSPORTATION SYSTEM 01)
MISSION DURATION   2 DAYS, 6 HOURS, 20 MINUTES
ORBITS   36
TOTAL LIFTOFF WEIGHT 4,457,111 LB (2,021,711 KG)
LANDING WEIGHT   195,472 LB (88,664 KG)
CREW   COMMANDER: JOHN YOUNG
        PILOT: ROBERT CRIPPEN

FIRST FLIGHT

Six years had passed since the last US astronauts were launched into space. NASA's vaunted Shuttle was two years late in its development, and had been much more difficult and expensive to prepare than managers had expected. So when commander John Young and pilot Robert Crippen strapped themselves into *Columbia*'s cabin for launch on April 10, 1981, tensions were high for everyone watching.

Inside the crew cabin, five computers cross-checked results to guarantee accuracy. For safety reasons, at least four of them had to match before *Columbia* could fly. But 20 minutes before the scheduled liftoff time, the onboard computers could not agree. Young and Crippen had to turn their spacecraft over to the engineers.

Two days later, pilot and commander once again climbed into their bulky, uncomfortable ejection seats. These seats would be replaced with seven crew couches once the Shuttle had proved itself to be reliable. On the first test flight, though, everyone was glad that the seats were there.

RETURN TO SPACE

At last, just after 7 a.m. on April 12, *Columbia* got off the launchpad and ascended flawlessly to orbit. America was back in space, and public reaction to the flight was tremendous. More than one million spectators thronged the beaches and fields beyond the Kennedy Space Center to watch the liftoff as it happened.

Once in orbit, Young and Crippen benefited from *Columbia*'s large cabin, which was much roomier than previous space capsules. There was even a second deck beneath the cockpit, with food storage, spacesuit racks, an air lock, and a private washroom cubicle.

Two days later, *Columbia*

GROUNDED

COLUMBIA WAS NOT THE FIRST SHUTTLE. IN 1977, THE *ENTERPRISE* WAS CARRIED ALOFT BY A SPECIAL BOEING 747 AND THEN DROPPED FOR GLIDE AND LANDING TESTS. BUT *ENTERPRISE* NEVER FLEW IN SPACE.

MISSION DIARY: SHUTTLE MISSION STS-1

APRIL 12, 1981, 07:00:03 A.M. EST COLUMBIA'S THREE MAIN ENGINES ARE IGNITED, FUELED BY LIQUID HYDROGEN AND LIQUID OXYGEN (RIGHT).
7:00:09 A.M. THE TWIN SOLID ROCKET BOOSTERS FIRE. THE SPACE SHUTTLE LIFTS OFF THE LAUNCHPAD.
7:02:10 A.M. THE SOLID BOOSTERS COMPLETE THEIR BURN. *COLUMBIA* IS NOW AT A 31-MILE (50 KM) ALTITUDE. THE BOOSTERS FALL AWAY. LATER, THEY ARE RECOVERED FROM THE SEA AND REUSED.
7:08:38 A.M. COLUMBIA'S MAIN ENGINES SHUT DOWN AT AN ALTITUDE OF 72 MILES (116 KM). THE EXTERNAL FUEL TANK IS DISCARDED AND FALLS INTO THE SEA.
7:10:37 A.M. COLUMBIA FIRES TWO SMALL ORBITAL MANEUVERING SYSTEM (OMS) ENGINES TO COMPLETE THE ASCENT TO ORBIT. THE SPACECRAFT NOW HAS AN

ALTITUDE OF 152 MILES (245 KM), AND A VELOCITY OF 17,322 MPH (27,877 KMH).
7:52 A.M. THE CARGO BAY DOORS ARE OPENED (BELOW LEFT) TO EXPOSE SOLAR PANELS THAT HELP POWER THE SHUTTLE'S EQUIPMENT. YOUNG AND CRIPPEN BEGIN TWO DAYS OF SYSTEMS TESTING.
1:20:49 P.M. ANOTHER OMS BURN CHANGES *COLUMBIA*'S ORBIT TO AN ALTITUDE OF 170 MILES (273 KM).
APRIL 14, 12:21:34 P.M. THE OMS ENGINES SLOW *COLUMBIA*, AND IT BEGINS FALLING TOWARD EARTH. AFTER 17 MINUTES, THE SHUTTLE BEGINS TO HEAT UP FROM REENTRY FRICTION.
1:20:56 P.M. COLUMBIA TOUCHES DOWN ON THE RUNWAY (BELOW) AT EDWARDS AIR FORCE BASE IN CALIFORNIA.

plunged back into the Earth's atmosphere and glided toward Edwards Air Force Base. It was a critical moment. With no engine power available, the pilots had to land the first time around. To NASA—and America's—huge

relief, they made a perfect touchdown.

Finally NASA had a vehicle that could deliver humans and cargo into space, and then be refurbished. Behind the crew cabin was a payload bay 60 feet

(18 m) long and 15 feet (4.5 m) wide. One day soon it would carry pressurized space laboratories, or large probes and satellites for release into space.

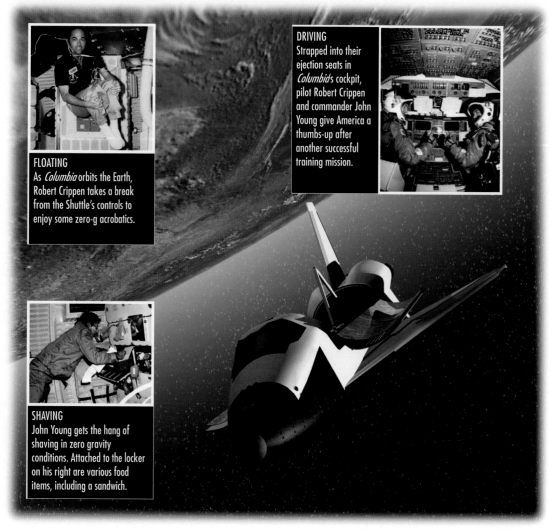

FLOATING
As *Columbia* orbits the Earth, Robert Crippen takes a break from the Shuttle's controls to enjoy some zero-g acrobatics.

DRIVING
Strapped into their ejection seats in *Columbia*'s cockpit, pilot Robert Crippen and commander John Young give America a thumbs-up after another successful training mission.

SHAVING
John Young gets the hang of shaving in zero gravity conditions. Attached to the locker on his right are various food items, including a sandwich.

SPACELAB

S pacelab was born in the early 1970s of a collaboration between two of the world's leading space agencies. NASA had the go-ahead for the Space Shuttle but was denied funding for a space station to go with it. The European Space Agency (ESA) wanted to send scientists into space but had no means of getting them there. The answer was to build a laboratory module that could be fitted inside the Shuttle's payload bay. First launched in 1983, Spacelab was a great success and heralded the age of space science.

SPACELAB STATS

Max. weight 32,000 lb (14,500 kg)	Missions 15 (crewed module), 6 (igloo/pallets)	Tunnel Length 8.7/18.9 ft (2.65/5.7 ft)
Participating ESA nations Belgium, Denmark, France, Germany, Ireland, Italy, Netherlands, Spain, Switzerland, UK	Core Module/Experiment Segment (pressurized)	Diameter 3.3 ft (1 m)
	Length 9 ft (2.7 m)	Instrument Pointing System
	Diameter 13.5 ft (4 m)	Weight 2,600 lb (1,180 kg)
Builders		Payload 6,600 lb (2,993 lb)
ERNO-VFW Fokker consortium (pressurized modules), British Aerospace (pallets), SABCA (igloo), Dornier (IPS), McDonnell-Douglas (tunnel)	Pallet (experiments only)	Igloo (instruments only)
	Length 10 ft (3 m)	Height 7.9 ft (2.4 m)
	Diameter 13.1 ft (4 m)	Diameter 3.6 ft (1.1 m)
	Weight 1,600 lb (725 kg)	Weight 1,400 lb (635 kg)
	Payload 3 tons (2.72 t) maximum	

SCIENCE LAB IN ORBIT

NASA's primary objectives after the Apollo Moon landings were to develop a reusable launch vehicle and to have human beings living and working in space for long periods of time. The government agreed to the first objective and gave a green light to the Space Shuttle program. But after Skylab, there was to be no money for the second aim. If NASA wanted a space station, it would have to go somewhere else to find it.

NASA went to Europe. In 1973, it signed an agreement with the European Space Agency (ESA) to develop a scientific research lab that could be carried into space in the Shuttle's payload bay. The result was

Spacelab, the first major US-European collaboration in space and Europe's first chance to put humans in orbit.

The Spacelab system is a set of modules that can be used in different combinations, depending on the kind of work to be done. The core segment is a pressurized laboratory, linked to the Orbiter's crew compartment by a 3-foot (1 m) -wide tunnel. The lab is fitted with a workbench and equipment racks, each loaded with up to 645 pounds (292 kg) of experiments. Usually, an almost identical experiment segment is bolted on to the core segment to extend the lab space. Each segment has a hole in the roof that can be fitted with either a window for photography or an air lock for

exposing experiments to open space. Oxygen, power, heat, and communications with Earth are all provided by the Shuttle.

ON THE OUTSIDE

The other components of the Spacelab system are designed to operate by remote control in open space. They consist of a set of ten U-shaped structures called pallets that mount scientific equipment in the Orbiter's payload bay. Some Spacelab missions are designated "pallets-only" and do without the pressurized lab segments. On such missions, up to five pallets can be carried, and the experiments are controlled by mission specialists from a console at the back of the Orbiter's flight deck. The control systems and utilities that normally

reside in the core segment are housed in the cargo bay inside a pressurized, temperature-controlled enclosure called the igloo.

Spacelab was not an independent space station like Skylab or Mir, and while in orbit it remained firmly clamped in the Shuttle's cargo bay. Yet its low-key missions were important all the same. Along with its partner Shuttles, Spacelab proved that space technology can be reusable—each module was designed to last fifty missions. Spacelab's greatest legacy, though, is likely to be the experience gained by visiting humans, not with hardware. Each flight took one to four civilian scientists into orbit, where only career astronauts had gone before. It was a significant step toward the large-scale habitation of space.

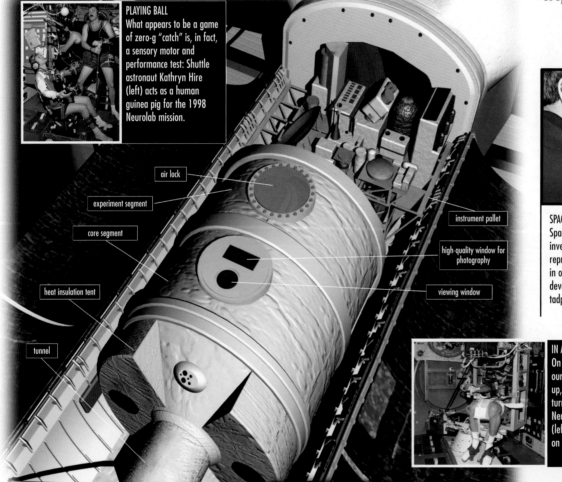

PLAYING BALL
What appears to be a game of zero-g "catch" is, in fact, a sensory motor and performance test: Shuttle astronaut Kathryn Hire (left) acts as a human guinea pig for the 1998 Neurolab mission.

air lock

experiment segment

core segment

heat insulation tent

tunnel

instrument pallet

high-quality window for photography

viewing window

SPACE FROGS
Spacelab took frogs into space in 1992 to investigate the effects of microgravity on reproduction and growth. The frogs laid eggs in orbit and scientists studied the development of the resulting embryos and tadpoles with interest.

IN A SPIN
On Earth, the movement of fluids in our ear tells the brain when we speed up, slow down, change direction, or turn upside down. As part of the Neurolab mission, an astronaut is spun (left) to test the effects of microgravity on this complex process.

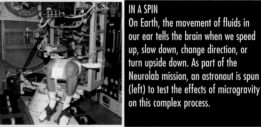

ON TARGET
An instrument pointing system (left) keeps Spacelab's telescopes and other instruments accurately trained on their targets or steers them through precision scans of the night sky. The crew control it directly or leave the work to computers guided by Sun sensors and star trackers.

FLYING THE SHUTTLE

Capturing a faulty satellite ... Docking with a space station to bring new crews and equipment ... Operating a space laboratory ... Servicing a space telescope ... Such activities were routine for the astronauts involved in the Space Shuttle program. Classed as a partially reusable manned spaceplane, the Shuttle was the most versatile spacecraft ever built. Even though it completed scores of missions since its maiden flight in 1981, Shuttle launches received live TV coverage and regularly attracted thousands of spectators to the Kennedy Space Center until its retirement in 2011.

SHUTTLE MISSIONS

ENTERPRISE (OV-101) WAS A TEST VEHICLE AND WAS NOT INTENDED FOR SPACE MISSIONS.

CHALLENGER (OV-99) FLEW TEN MISSIONS FROM 1983 TO 1986. SHE WAS LOST APPROXIMATELY 73 SECONDS AFTER TAKEOFF ON MISSION STS-51-L IN 1986.

ATLANTIS (OV-104) FLEW TWENTY-SIX MISSIONS FROM 1985 TO 2002, AND REMAINED IN SERVICE UNTIL 2011.

ENDEAVOUR (OV-105) FLEW NINETEEN MISSIONS FROM 1992 TO 2002. ENDEAVOUR REMAINED IN SERVICE UNTIL 2011.

COLUMBIA (OV-102) FLEW TWENTY-EIGHT MISSIONS FROM 1981-2003, INCLUDING STS-1, THE VERY FIRST SHUTTLE MISSION. SHE WAS LOST SHORTLY BEFORE TOUCHDOWN ON MISSION STS-107.

DISCOVERY (OV-103) HAS FLOWN THIRTY-ONE MISSIONS FROM 1984 TO THE PRESENT. DISCOVERY MADE THE FIRST RETURN-TO-FLIGHT MISSION AFTER THE LOSS OF COLOMBIA IN AUGUST 2005.

SPACE WAGON

The Space Shuttle was a general-purpose space truck, whose job was to ferry people and cargo to and from orbit above the Earth. Given its limitations, it performed its task with remarkable efficiency.

The Shuttle was launched like a conventional rocket, which jettisoned its twin reusable solid-fuel boosters two minutes after liftoff. The Orbiter spaceplane then climbed under the power of its own rocket engines, which were fed with liquid propellant from a giant external fuel tank. Six minutes later the Shuttle reached orbit and shed its tank, which then burned up in the Earth's atmosphere. Shortly after this, astronauts and payload specialists were able to begin their work.

WORKING IN SPACE

The Orbiter's payload bay contained satellites, repair equipment, or pressurized modules for conducting space experiments. Some payloads are

deployed by remote control; others are operated directly by the crew who are able to access the payload bay via a tunnel.

Shuttle missions usually lasted an average of nine days, though some extended to three weeks. The crew then had to live and work in the cramped flight deck or lower mid-deck—which also

serves as a galley, sleeping quarters, and bathroom. Some missions were divided into shifts to allow for twenty-four-hour work days.

On completion of a mission, the Shuttle's engines redirected it back to Earth. After a bumpy ride through the atmosphere, protected by its heat shield tiles,

it came in to land like an airplane. Always a popular craft, the Shuttle was only retired after thirty years' service.

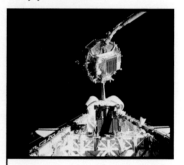

RETRIEVAL
A Japanese satellite is retrieved (above) from orbit by the robot arm of the Shuttle *Endeavour* on January 13, 1996. The square object in the foreground, another satellite, was launched during the same mission on January 15 and was retrieved two days later.

WHAT THE SHUTTLE DID

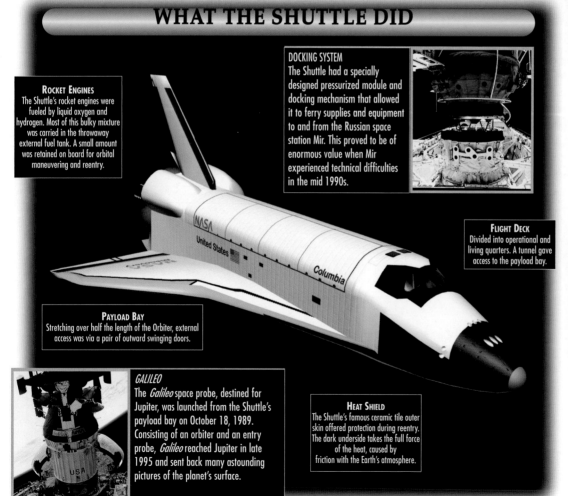

ROCKET ENGINES
The Shuttle's rocket engines were fueled by liquid oxygen and hydrogen. Most of this bulky mixture was carried in the throwaway external fuel tank. A small amount was retained on board for orbital maneuvering and reentry.

DOCKING SYSTEM
The Shuttle had a specially designed pressurized module and docking mechanism that allowed it to ferry supplies and equipment to and from the Russian space station Mir. This proved to be of enormous value when Mir experienced technical difficulties in the mid 1990s.

FLIGHT DECK
Divided into operational and living quarters. A tunnel gave access to the payload bay.

PAYLOAD BAY
Stretching over half the length of the Orbiter, external access was via a pair of outward swinging doors.

GALILEO
The *Galileo* space probe, destined for Jupiter, was launched from the Shuttle's payload bay on October 18, 1989. Consisting of an orbiter and an entry probe, *Galileo* reached Jupiter in late 1995 and sent back many astounding pictures of the planet's surface.

HEAT SHIELD
The Shuttle's famous ceramic tile outer skin offered protection during reentry. The dark underside takes the full force of the heat, caused by friction with the Earth's atmosphere.

SPACELAB
This was the name given to the Shuttle's original pressurized laboratory module. Spacelab is primarily used by US and European engineers, scientists, and astronauts to study the long-term effects of weightlessness on living things.

CHALLENGER DISASTER

There was an almost carnival atmosphere at the Kennedy Space Center, Florida, on January 28, 1986, as crowds gathered for the twenty-fifth flight of the Space Shuttle. On board the Shuttle Orbiter *Challenger* was the first "ordinary American citizen," a teacher named Christa McAuliffe, whose cheerful personality had already endeared her to the public. After a long series of delays, at 11:38 EST the Shuttle lifted off the launchpad into a clear, blue sky. Tragically, only 73 seconds later, *Challenger* was gone.

THE *CHALLENGER* CREW

BACK ROW, LEFT TO RIGHT
ELLISON SHOJI ONIZUKA (MISSION SPECIALIST), BORN JUNE 14, 1946
SHARON CHRISTA CORRIGAN MCAULIFFE (PAYLOAD SPECIALIST),
BORN SEPTEMBER 2, 1948
GREGORY BRUCE JARVIS (PAYLOAD SPECIALIST), BORN AUGUST 24, 1944
JUDITH ARLENE RESNIK (MISSION SPECIALIST), BORN APRIL 5, 1949

FRONT ROW, LEFT TO RIGHT
MICHAEL JOHN SMITH (PILOT), COMMANDER US NAVY,
BORN APRIL 30, 1945
FRANCIS RICHARD SCOBEE (COMMANDER), BORN MAY 19, 1939
RONALD ERWIN MCNAIR (MISSION SPECIALIST), BORN OCTOBER 21, 1950

FATAL FLAW

NASA intended 1986 to be a landmark year for the space program. The Space Shuttle was to make fifteen flights, and President Reagan was confidently expected to give the go-ahead for the project that would see a US space station in orbit by 1994. It needed to be a good year. Mission 61-C *Columbia* had been progressively delayed from the year before, public interest in space was on the wane, and rumors were circulating in the media of repeated NASA incompetence. Its reputation as the foremost space agency in the world was beginning to slip.

It seemed that if anything could restore government and public confidence, it would be Shuttle launch 51-L *Challenger*. NASA saw to it that the inclusion of the first woman civilian astronaut, schoolteacher Christa McAuliffe, received maximum media coverage. The nation warmed to her—and to the idea that ordinary people might be going into space.

WAITING TO HAPPEN

Behind the scenes, there was growing concern among NASA technicians about the safety of the Shuttle. The focus of this concern was the flexible sealing system of putty and synthetic-rubber O-rings used on the "field joints" between sections of the reusable solid rocket boosters (SRBs). In-flight damage to the seals had been noticed on previous missions, implying a design fault, but no action was taken to solve the problem.

With *Challenger* already behind schedule after delays in

the *Columbia* mission, the pressure mounted for a swift launch. The crew finally boarded on January 27, only to be told, just 30 minutes from liftoff, that the mission was postponed due to a hatch fault. Meanwhile, engineers at Morton Thiokol, makers of the SRBs, voiced serious concerns about the effects of cold weather on the O-

ring seals, which might weaken them more. A severe cold front was forecast to hit Florida the following day that would see temperatures plummet to 23°F (–5°C). The engineers suggested postponing the launch until the cold snap passed, but their suggestion was overruled by NASA officials and the launch went ahead.

One week later, as the nation mourned its dead, President Reagan assigned a commission to investigate the cause of the accident. Their report, published on June 6, 1986, stated that the cause "was the failure of the pressure seal in the aft field joint of the right-hand solid rocket booster ... due to a faulty design ..."

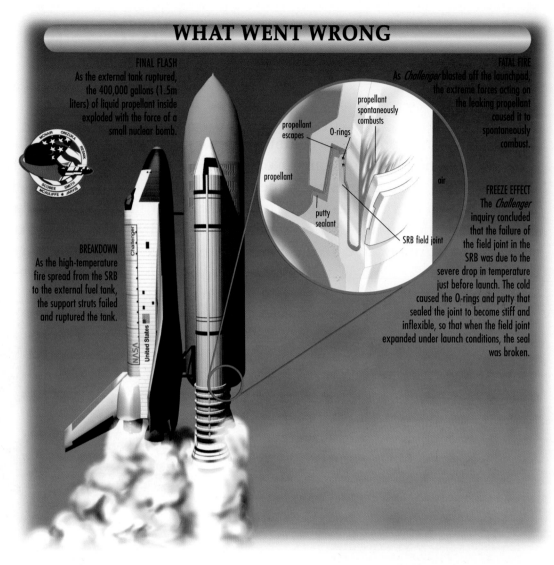

WHAT WENT WRONG

FINAL FLASH
As the external tank ruptured, the 400,000 gallons (1.5m liters) of liquid propellant inside exploded with the force of a small nuclear bomb.

BREAKDOWN
As the high-temperature fire spread from the SRB to the external fuel tank, the support struts failed and ruptured the tank.

propellant escapes
propellant spontaneously combusts
O-rings
propellant
putty sealant
air
SRB field joint

FATAL FIRE
As *Challenger* blasted off the launchpad, the extreme forces acting on the leaking propellant caused it to spontaneously combust.

FREEZE EFFECT
The *Challenger* inquiry concluded that the failure of the field joint in the SRB was due to the severe drop in temperature just before launch. The cold caused the O-rings and putty that sealed the joint to become stiff and inflexible, so that when the field joint expanded under launch conditions, the seal was broken.

MISSION DIARY: COUNTDOWN TO DISASTER

T+0.6 SEC A LAUNCH CAMERA PHOTOGRAPHS PUFFS OF SMOKE LOW-DOWN ON THE RIGHT-HAND SOLID ROCKET BOOSTER. THE SMOKE IS THE FIRST SIGN OF THE PROPELLANT THAT HAS BEGUN TO LEAK FROM A FAULTY O-RING SEAL IN THE AFT FIELD JOINT.
T+35 SEC AFTER A SEEMINGLY PERFECT LAUNCH, THE *CHALLENGER*'S MAIN ENGINES ARE THROTTLED DOWN TO 65 PERCENT AS THE CRAFT ENTERS THE PERIOD OF MAXIMUM DYNAMIC PRESSURE.
T+37 SEC SEVERE FLUCTUATIONS IN THE FLIGHT PATH BEGIN; THESE CONTINUE FOR ANOTHER 26 SECONDS AND ARE LATER ATTRIBUTED TO "WIND SHEAR"—AN EXPLANATION QUESTIONED BY MANY

ANALYSTS.
T+51 SEC ENGINES ARE SET TO FULL THROTTLE.
T+58 SEC FLAMES

APPEAR AROUND THE FAULTY FIELD JOINT (CIRCLED, ABOVE). BY THIS TIME THE O-RING SEAL HAS FAILED COMPLETELY.
T+60 SEC THE FLAMES SPREAD RAPIDLY OVER THE STRUTS THAT SECURE THE SRBs AND THE EXTERNAL FUEL TANK (ET).
T+64 SEC THE ET IS BREACHED, BRINGING THE FLAMES INTO CONTACT WITH THE LIQUID HYDROGEN THAT IS LEAKING FROM THE TANK.

T+72 SEC IN A RAPID SEQUENCE OF EVENTS: THE STRUT LINKING THE RIGHT-HAND SRB TO THE ET FRACTURES; THE AFT DOME FALLS AWAY, RIPPING PARTS OF THE TANK APART; THEN THE SEVERED SRB HITS THE ET, CAUSING LIQUID OXYGEN TO MIX WITH LIQUID HYDROGEN IN A LETHAL COCKTAIL.
T+73 SEC THE MIXTURE OF LEAKING LIQUID FUELS ERUPTS IN AN EXPLOSION (RIGHT). THE ET DISINTEGRATES AND BOTH SRBs FLY OFF OUT OF CONTROL, LATER TO BE REMOTE-DETONATED BY THE RANGE SAFETY OFFICER. THE ORBITER IS BLOWN CLEAR BUT INSTANTLY BREAKS UP DUE TO AERODYNAMIC FORCES. THE ONBOARD FUEL EXPLODES, THROWING THE

CABIN CLEAR OF THE FIREBALL AND LEAVING THE WRECKAGE TO PLUNGE INTO THE ATLANTIC OCEAN. IT IS BELIEVED THAT SOME OF THE CREW INITIALLY SURVIVED THE EXPLOSION.

MIR

Mir was the first permanent space station, a unique complex specifically designed for expansion. Originally of Soviet origin, visiting spacecraft from a variety of nations could attach as many as nine modules to it. With many docking compartments to choose from, no one could predict what would be added, or when, or where. In the end, the space station looked like the product of a bizarre engineering experiment in zero gravity. Despite the many problems and near disasters Mir suffered, its relay of crews made it work astonishingly well—and for far longer than was originally

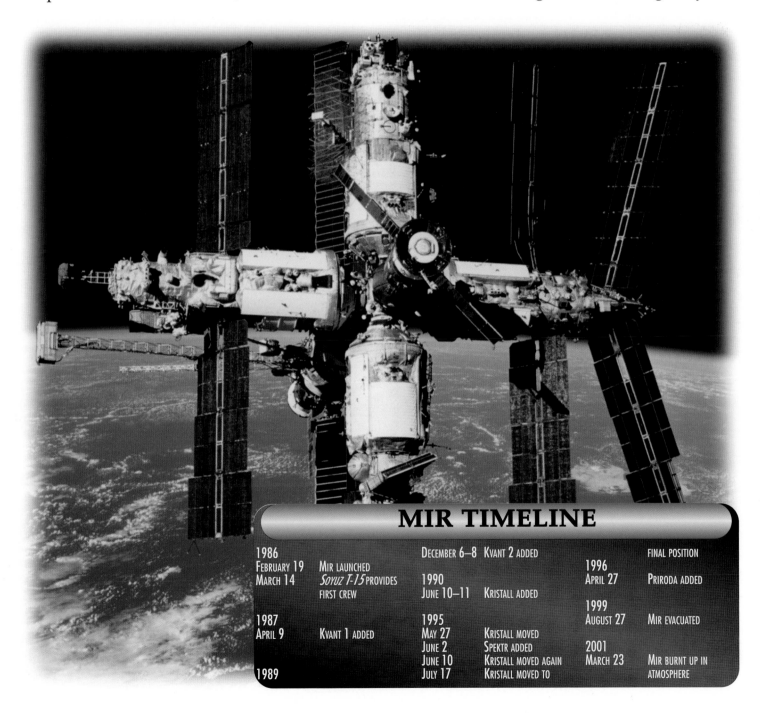

MIR TIMELINE

1986		
February 19	Mir launched	
March 14	*Soyuz T-15* provides first crew	
1987		
April 9	Kvant 1 added	
1989		
December 6–8	Kvant 2 added	
1990		
June 10–11	Kristall added	
1995		
May 27	Kristall moved	
June 2	Spektr added	
June 10	Kristall moved again	
July 17	Kristall moved to final position	
1996		
April 27	Priroda added	
1999		
August 27	Mir evacuated	
2001		
March 23	Mir burnt up in atmosphere	

COSMIC JALOPY

During its fourteen-year existence, Mir grew from a single core unit to a complex of six. At its heart was the central module, with a work room, an intermediate room, and an adapter: a spherical 7-foot (2.1 m) unit with five docking ports. Cosmonauts lived and worked in the main room, 43 feet (13 m) long and 13.6 feet (4 m) across. It contained the control station, physical fitness machinery, cabins, and two tables with special compartments for working in zero gravity.

In April 1987, after two crewed missions ensured that Mir was in good running order, it acquired its first addition—Kvant, an astrophysics research module. Without engines of its own, Kvant had a little "tug" that maneuvered it in orbit to its

docking port. Instruments on the 19-foot (5.7 m), 22-ton (20 t) module included an X-ray observatory and powerful gyroscopes that would keep the station stable, so that the telescopes could remain fixed on faint objects.

Over the next two years and eight months, Mir-Kvant received twenty visits, several of them from international-crewed space missions. Progress craft—uncrewed space ferries—arrived every month or two, to bring new supplies and carry away trash.

The next add-on unit, Kvant 2, arrived in December 1989, turning Mir from a straight-line station into an L-shape. It brought extra power to make Mir more self-sufficient: the station could now remove carbon dioxide and recycle water vapor and urine to make oxygen.

HOME IMPROVEMENTS

In June 1990, the third module, Kristall, was attached. It was a specialist unit for research into the manufacture of materials for semiconductors. Its retractable and detachable solar panels upgraded the power supply.

But now Mir was reaching the limits of its capacity. Originally, it was to have been replaced around 1992 by Mir 2, but the Soviet Union's successor, Russia, had no cash for a replacement.

Only when the US agreed to make use of Mir in 1995 could Russia plan on the final units, Spektr and Priroda. The half-dozen Shuttle-Mir missions of 1995–7 gave the aging station a new injection of cash, as well as a new lease on life. In June 1995, Spektr was bolted on. Finally, in April 1996, Priroda, laden with a mass of environmental sensors,

became Mir's final addition. Together, the two modules gave the station a formidable ability to gather and correlate information about the Earth's environment.

But there were problems. In 1997, crews had to cope with a fire, a crash that knocked out one of Spektr's panels, and the near-collapse of power systems. The crises made it clear that it would take all the crews' time simply to keep Mir alive. Scientific work ceased and the last team abandoned ship on August 27, 1999. Despite occasional suggestions that Mir might somehow be rescued, it became obvious that the station's time was over. In 2001 the engines of the Progress supply rocket docked to the station were fired for the last time, braking the station so that it fell into Earth's atmosphere.

Much of the station burned up in the Earth's atmosphere, putting on a final spectacular show. Parts of the station—possibly as much as 25 tons (22.5 t)—fell into the Pacific Ocean in a target zone specifically chosen to eliminate any risk to people on the ground.

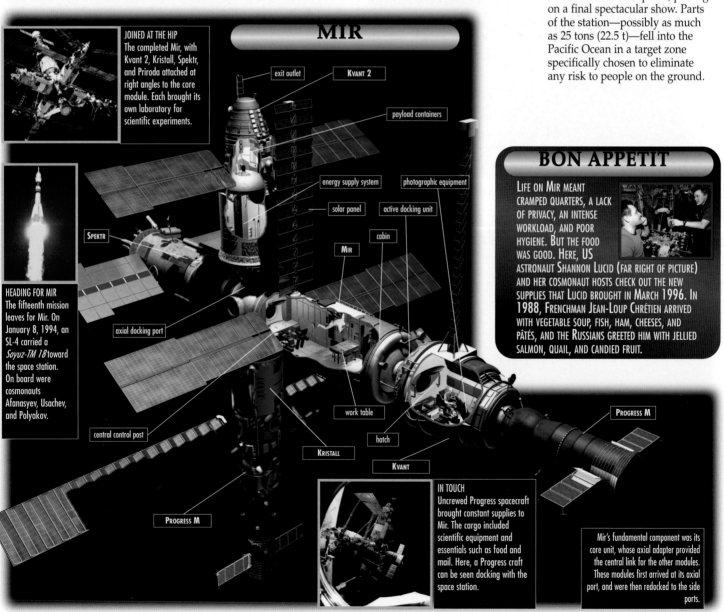

MIR

JOINED AT THE HIP The completed Mir, with Kvant 2, Kristall, Spektr, and Priroda attached at right angles to the core module. Each brought its own laboratory for scientific experiments.

HEADING FOR MIR The fifteenth mission leaves for Mir. On January 8, 1994, an SL-4 carried a *Soyuz-TM 18* toward the space station. On board were cosmonauts Afanasyev, Usachev, and Polyakov.

exit outlet

KVANT 2

payload containers

energy supply system

photographic equipment

solar panel

active docking unit

SPEKTR

cabin

MIR

axial docking port

central control post

PROGRESS M

work table

hatch

KRISTALL

KVANT

PROGRESS M

IN TOUCH Uncrewed Progress spacecraft brought constant supplies to Mir. The cargo included scientific equipment and essentials such as food and mail. Here, a Progress craft can be seen docking with the space station.

BON APPETIT

LIFE ON MIR MEANT CRAMPED QUARTERS, A LACK OF PRIVACY, AN INTENSE WORKLOAD, AND POOR HYGIENE. BUT THE FOOD WAS GOOD. HERE, US ASTRONAUT SHANNON LUCID (FAR RIGHT OF PICTURE) AND HER COSMONAUT HOSTS CHECK OUT THE NEW SUPPLIES THAT LUCID BROUGHT IN MARCH 1996. IN 1988, FRENCHMAN JEAN-LOUP CHRÉTIEN ARRIVED WITH VEGETABLE SOUP, FISH, HAM, CHEESES, AND PÂTÉS, AND THE RUSSIANS GREETED HIM WITH JELLIED SALMON, QUAIL, AND CANDIED FRUIT.

Mir's fundamental component was its core unit, whose axial adapter provided the central link for the other modules. These modules first arrived at its axial port, and were then redocked to the side ports.

INTERNATIONAL
SPACE STATION

The International Space Station (ISS) is the biggest space structure ever built. In its low Earth orbit (LEO), 220 miles (355 km) up, it is easy to see in the night sky. The ISS was designed to be assembled in orbit from components flown up on Space Shuttle flights and Russian Proton and Soyuz missions. The station provides living quarters, workshops, and laboratories for astronauts from the US and nations around the world and can be upgraded and adapted with the replacement or addition of modules.

ISS SPECIFICATIONS

CREW	3 (INITIAL) 7 (FINAL)	PLANNED LIFE	9+ YEARS AFTER FINAL ASSEMBLY
MASS	475 TONS (430 T)	ASSEMBLY COST	$37 BILLION
DIMENSIONS	356 FT X 290 FT (108 X 88 M) (INCLUDING SOLAR ARRAYS)	OPERATING COST	$13 BILLION FOR 9 YEARS OF OPERATIONS
		COUNTRIES INVOLVED	US, RUSSIA, JAPAN, CANADA, BRAZIL, FRANCE, GERMANY, ITALY, BELGIUM, DENMARK, THE NETHERLANDS, NORWAY, SPAIN, SWEDEN, SWITZERLAND
ORBIT	220 MILES (355 KM), INCLINED 51.6° TO EQUATOR		
TIME TO ASSEMBLE	6 YEARS (INCLUDING 930 HRS OF US SPACEWALK TIME)		

SCIENCE IN ORBIT

The crew of a Space Shuttle arriving at the newly completed International Space Station (ISS) are greeted by a massive structure 356 feet (108 m) long and 290 feet (88 m) wide, nearly the size of two football fields.

Clustered at the center of this sprawling space complex are the modules containing laboratories, workshops, and the living quarters for up to seven crew members. The work of the crew involves scientific, medical, and technological research that can only be carried out in the near-weightless conditions of orbit in space. It includes studies of the human body to search for new ways of preventing and treating diseases, and the development of new types of materials, including semiconductor crystals, plastics, and drugs.

The station is also an excellent platform for observing the Earth because its orbit takes it over 85 percent of the planet's surface. From their high vantage point, scientists study weather patterns, land usage, the spread of deserts, and the destruction of rain forests.

Crews are taken to and from the ISS by US Space Shuttles and Russian Soyuz ferry craft. Supplies and propellants are delivered by Shuttle flights and by unmanned ferries including Russian Progress vehicles, the European ATV, and the Japanese HTV.

LIFE-SUPPORT SYSTEMS

On board the station, the life-support systems maintain comfortable "shirt-sleeve" conditions for the comfort of the crew. Water is used for drinking and washing and is also electrolyzed to produce oxygen for breathing. This oxygen is mixed with nitrogen to create a fair approximation of the air on Earth.

The temperature and humidity of the air are regulated by air conditioners, and the air is circulated around the ISS by fans. Molecular sieves remove carbon dioxide from it, and activated charcoal filters and catalytic oxidizers scrub away contaminants. Waste water from the air conditioners, sinks, showers, and toilets is recycled for drinking.

The main hazards of life in low Earth orbit are radiation, space debris, and micrometeorites. During periods of maximum solar activity, when solar flares create high levels of radiation, the crews "hide" in the best-shielded parts of the station.

The modules are built to withstand impacts of space debris and meteorite particles up to half an inch (12 millimeter) in size. The US modules, for instance, are made from 1.25-inch (30 mm) aluminum with layers of Nextel impact protection material and thermal insulation—making the walls about 3 inches (75 mm) thick in total. Particles larger than 4 inches (100 mm) across can be tracked from Earth, and, given enough warning, the ISS can maneuver to avoid a collision. But any impacts from particles between 0.5 inches (12 mm) and 4 inches (100 mm) in size are potentially dangerous.

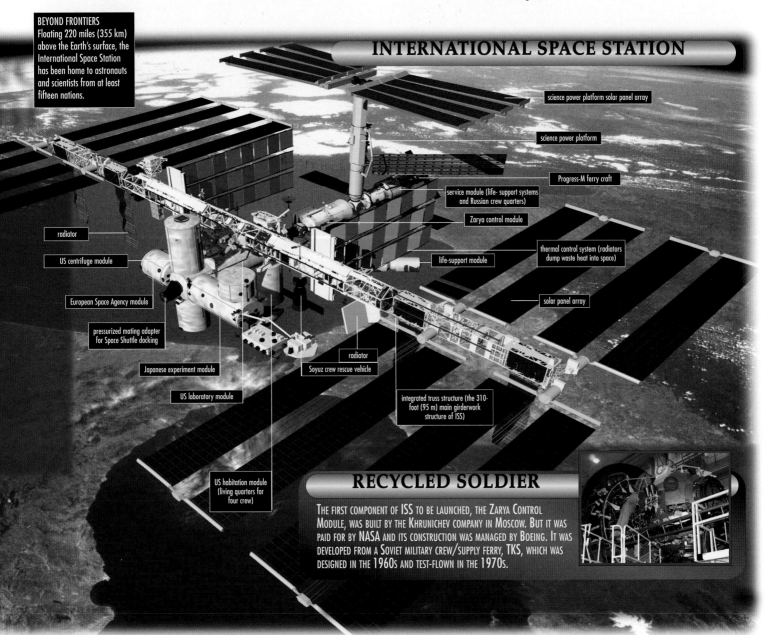

BEYOND FRONTIERS
Floating 220 miles (355 km) above the Earth's surface, the International Space Station has been home to astronauts and scientists from at least fifteen nations.

INTERNATIONAL SPACE STATION

science power platform solar panel array

science power platform

Progress-M ferry craft

service module (life-support systems and Russian crew quarters)

Zarya control module

thermal control system (radiators dump waste heat into space)

life-support module

solar panel array

radiator

US centrifuge module

European Space Agency module

pressurized mating adapter for Space Shuttle docking

radiator

Soyuz crew rescue vehicle

Japanese experiment module

US laboratory module

integrated truss structure (the 310-foot (95 m) main girderwork structure of ISS)

US habitation module (living quarters for four crew)

RECYCLED SOLDIER

THE FIRST COMPONENT OF ISS TO BE LAUNCHED, THE ZARYA CONTROL MODULE, WAS BUILT BY THE KHRUNICHEV COMPANY IN MOSCOW. BUT IT WAS PAID FOR BY NASA AND ITS CONSTRUCTION WAS MANAGED BY BOEING. IT WAS DEVELOPED FROM A SOVIET MILITARY CREW/SUPPLY FERRY, TKS, WHICH WAS DESIGNED IN THE 1960S AND TEST-FLOWN IN THE 1970S.

SHENZHOU 9

China's first manned spaceflight took place in June 2012, when *Shenzhou 9* was launched by a Chinese Long March 2F rocket from the Jiuquan Satellite Launch Center in Gansu Province. The spacecraft successfully docked with Tiangong-1, China's first space station module, on June 18, 2012, where it stayed for twelve days, carrying out various procedural experiments and testing the manual docking capabilities. The first Shenzhou craft—*Shenzhou 8*—was unmanned to trial these procedures. *Shenzhou 10*, which followed *Shenzhou 9*, also carried a manned crew of three to further prepare the astronauts for prolonged periods in space, as well as to carry out continued tests in the initial Space Station module.

SHENZHOU HISTORY

SPACECRAFT	TIME IN SPACE	MISSION AIM
1	21 HOURS	UNMANNED TEST FLIGHT
2	7 DAYS 10 HOURS	TEST FLIGHT WITH ANIMALS
3	6 DAYS 18 HOURS	TEST DUMMY FLIGHT AND OBSERVATION
4	6 DAYS 18 HOURS	TEST DUMMY AND SCIENTIFIC EXPERIMENTS CARRIED
5	21 HOURS	MANNED FLIGHT IN LEO WITH ONE CREW MEMBER
6	4 DAYS 19 HOURS	MANNED FLIGHT WITH TWO CREW MEMBERS
7	2 DAYS 20 HOURS	MANNED FLIGHT WITH THREE CREW MEMBERS, SPACEWALK PERFORMED
8	16 DAYS 13 HOURS	UNMANNED MISSION, DOCKED WITH TIANGONG-1
9	12 DAYS 15 HOURS	MANNED MISSION WITH THREE CREW MEMBERS, DOCKED WITH TIANGONG-1
10	15 DAYS	MANNED MISSION WITH THREE CREW MEMBERS, DOCKED WITH TIANGONG-1

BREAKING NEW BOUNDARIES

Featuring China's first female astronaut and launching forty-nine years to the day after Valentina Tereshkova—the first ever female cosmonaut—went to space, *Shenzhou 9* was the first manned spacecraft to dock with the Tiangong-1 space station on June 18, 2012. *Shenzhou 9* followed *Shenzhou 8*, an unmanned craft that had been the first to dock with Tiangong-1 in November 2012, thereby testing its automatic docking capabilities. On June 15, the crew were introduced to the world press, as well as an eager China. While there had been two prospective female astronauts for the mission, Liu Yang alone was eventually chosen as the first Chinese female to enter space. Joining her were crew members Jing Haipeng, the first repeat Chinese astronaut, who commanded the mission,

and the pilot, Liu Wang. Liu Yang was a member of the People's Liberation Army Air Force, where she clocked over 1,600 hours of flight experience. She trained for two years as an astronaut before being selected for the *Shenzhou 9* mission. During the mission, Yang was responsible for carrying out experiments in space medicine. As yet, Yang has not returned to space.

Shenzhou 9 was the ninth flight of the Shenzhou program—which was conceived in 1992 and put China's first citizen into space on October 15, 2003—and its fourth manned spaceflight. Shenzhou spacecraft follow the basic design of the Russian Soyuz series. There are three modules, comprised of an orbital module, a reentry capsule, and a service module. The crafts are bigger than the Soyuz series, and might in the future be even larger to accomodate four astronauts instead of three.

Shenzhou 9 and its three astronauts landed safely back to Earth on June 29, 2012. The craft's modules separated on the June 28, allowing only the reentry capsule to enter a trajectory on course for the landing site in Inner Mongolia. After the reentry, the craft's parachute deployed to slow the fall, which was combined with ignition of the rockets to further reduce touchdown speed. Although *Shenzhou 9* flipped once on landing, all crew members landed safely and in good health. With the *Shenzhou 10* mission being equally successful, the future looks bright for China's presence in space over the next ten years.

WANG YAPING
China's second female astronaut, Wang Yaping, is shown here in one of the many promotional images returned from *Shenzhou 10.* She is also a captain in the People's Liberation Army Air Force.

PRESENT AND FUTURE

Shenzhou 10 followed *9* by also docking with Tiangong-1. It was launched on June 11, 2013, and docked with the space station after two days in orbit. *Shenzhou 10*'s crew featured Wang Yaping, China's second female astronaut, as well as two male astronauts. The crew performed a series of experiments in the space station's laboratory and followed on from *Shenzhou 9*'s experiments by testing space medicines—as well as practicing successful docking tests, spending a total of fifteen days aboard the space station. Wang Yaping also gave a science lecture from Tiangong-1 that was broadcast to approximately 60 million Chinese students. Her lecture included five experiments that she carried out for everyone to see, including showing how water droplets form a ball when in space. There are currently no more Shenzhou missions underway.

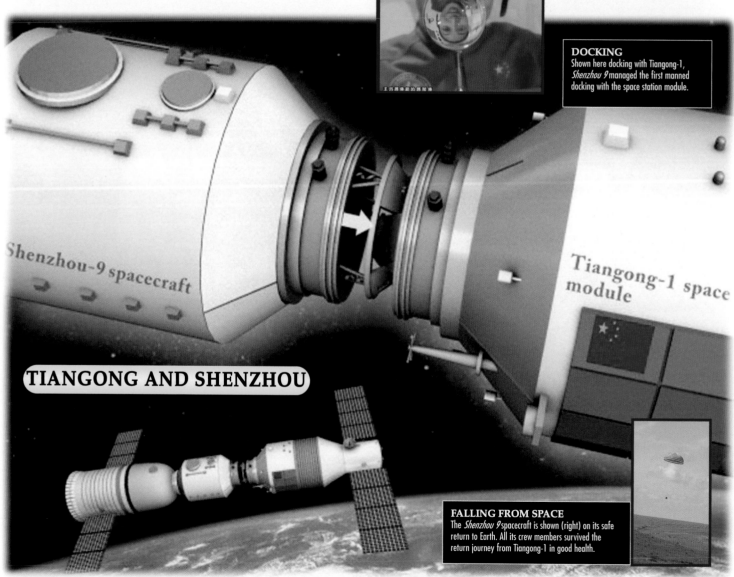

TIANGONG AND SHENZHOU

Shenzhou-9 spacecraft

Tiangong-1 space module

DOCKING
Shown here docking with Tiangong-1, *Shenzhou 9* managed the first manned docking with the space station module.

FALLING FROM SPACE
The *Shenzhou 9* spacecraft is shown (right) on its safe return to Earth. All its crew members survived the return journey from Tiangong-1 in good health.

TO THE MOON

Jules Verne imagined the first Moon voyagers would arrive by cannon shell, but is sketchy on how they might have returned. Getting to the Moon may have seemed easy, but the first attempts by the United States and USSR to send probes to impact the Moon in the late 1950s ended ignominiously when the launchers failed. A manned orbiter—Apollo 8—was not to come until a decade later. At the same time the Russians were restricting themselves to unmanned orbiters, landers, and rovers. Their unmanned missions achieved just one sample return to Earth, while the Apollo program delivered a dozen men to the Moon, returning them and many lunar rock and soil samples to Earth.

Getting two men and some equipment to the Moon required one of the most complicated machines ever built, the Saturn 5 launcher and associated Command Module, Lunar Module, and Service Module, built by a variety of contractors. Over 90 percent of these expensive components were burned up, sent into eternal orbit, or abandoned on the Moon, with only a cramped capsule returning to splash down on Earth. Any future Moon mission, if not as efficient as Verne's one-way projectile, will have to be less wasteful, but no less an adventure.

SOVIET LUNAR PROGRAM

When President John F. Kennedy declared in 1961 that the United States was going to put a man on the Moon by the end of the decade, NASA burst into activity—ready to meet the challenge. But NASA was not alone in their efforts. The Soviet Union had decided that it was going to beat America to the Moon. Thus began a frantic race between the two superpowers to develop the necessary technology and expertise to be the first to put a man on the Moon. It was a race the Soviets did not plan to lose.

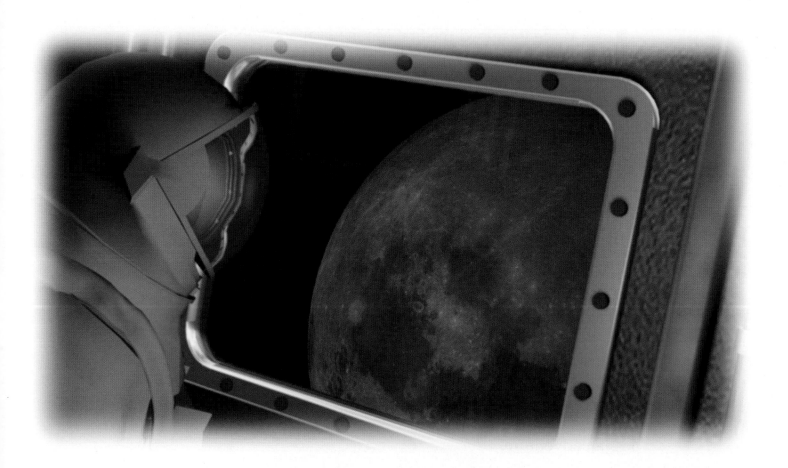

SOVIET STEPS TO THE MOON

JANUARY 30, 1956	POLITBURO HEARS PLANS FOR LANDING A COSMONAUT ON THE MOON	FEBRUARY 21, 1969	FIRST N-1 LAUNCH ATTEMPT FAILS
MAY 1962	N-1 VEHICLE DESIGN COMPLETE	JULY 3, 1969	SECOND N-1 LAUNCH ATTEMPT ENDS IN FAILURE
SEPTEMBER 24, 1962	POLITBURO AUTHORIZES CONSTRUCTION OF N-1	JUNE 27, 1971	THIRD N-1 LAUNCH ATTEMPT ENDS IN FAILURE
AUGUST 3, 1964	CENTRAL COMMITTEE ISSUES DECREE TO BEAT THE US TO THE MOON	NOVEMBER 23, 1972	FOURTH N-1 LAUNCH ATTEMPT ENDS IN FAILURE
SEPTEMBER 1965	ZOND 5 ORBITS MOON	MAY 1974	MISHIN REPLACED BY VALENTIN GLUSHKO, WHO ENDS LUNAR PROGRAM
JANUARY 14, 1966	SERGEI KOROLEV DIES, REPLACED BY VASILI MISHIN		

NEVER THE MOON

Though most people think the Moon race began with President Kennedy's famous 1961 speech, the Soviet Union had already been planning a crewed lunar landing for quite some time. The government's cabinet or Politburo had heard plans for such a mission on January 30, 1956. But the Soviets wasted valuable time. It was not until 1964—when they realized that the US was serious about its lunar ambitions—that the Central Committee issued a decree that would place a Soviet cosmonaut on the Moon before the Americans got there.

Unlike the United States, the Soviet Union did not have a single organization for space exploration. Premier Nikita Khrushchev believed that competition between rival bodies would create better designs. Three design bureaus had been working on plans to land on the Moon: OKB 1, run by Sergei Korolev, the man behind the triumphs of Sputnik and Yuri Gagarin; OKB 586, run by Michael Yangel; and OKB 52, run by Vladimir Chelomei. Each proposed, designed, and began building different vehicles for lunar missions. In the end, Korolev's Nositel ("carrier") 1 rocket, or N-1, was selected as the booster and his LOK as the orbiter, with Yangel's LK lander chosen for the descent to the surface. The first landing was planned for 1968.

The plans did not go smoothly. The original flight profile was to have several rockets lift different modules to rendezvous in low Earth orbit. The units would dock, transfer fuel and crew, then boost for the Moon. But this plan soon had to be modified.

Earth

outward trajectory

modified Soyuz spacecraft

LK module separates

LK fires Block D motor to begin descent

LK fires Block E motor to make landing

Block D motor jettisoned at 12,500 feet (3,810 m) from the Moon

LK touches down. Block E will also be used for liftoff

Block D impacts lunar surface

The LK lander would have traveled to the Moon mated to a modified Soyuz. Just one cosmonaut would spacewalk into the LK for the trip to the surface.

THE LK LANDER
The Soviet LK lander only had room for a single cosmonaut. It consisted of four modules: a detachable landing gear, an engine, a cabin pod with thrusters, and the docking mechanism.

THE N-1 ROCKET
The N-1 was the Soviet counterpart to NASA's Saturn 5 booster. Between February 1969 and November 1972, the Soviets tried to launch four N-1s. Unfortunately, each attempt ended in failure.

ONE-MAN MOONCRAFT

DEATH AND DOOM

Korolev, who became the project leader in late 1965, was convinced that the multiple-module approach was too difficult and did not favor Chelomei's designs. Instead, the design for the N-1 was changed, upgrading its payload capacity. The flight profile was changed to two launches, one for the lunar craft and another for the crew. Korolev was confident

that this plan would beat the Americans—but disaster struck.

On January 14, 1966, Korolev died unexpectedly while undergoing surgery. Without his genius behind the program, Soviet hopes were lost. Development of the N-1 booster was quickly bogged down in technical problems and redesigns, taking time the Soviets could ill afford to lose.

The N-1 finally lifted off from

Baikonur on February 21, 1969— and exploded 66 seconds later. Soviet engineers modified a second N-1 and quickly prepared it for launch. The lander was not ready, but OKB 1 scientists hoped to get a lunar flyaround under their belt. On July 3 the rocket exploded at launch. The blast obliterated the launchpad. Thirteen days later NASA launched Apollo 11. The race was over.

MISSION DIARY: THE STORY OF THE N-1

APRIL 12, 1961 YURI GAGARIN BECOMES THE FIRST PERSON IN SPACE IN A VOSTOK CAPSULE (VOSTOK REPLICA, RIGHT).
1966 START OF LUNAR COSMONAUT TRAINING.
NOVEMBER 1966 THE FIRST N-1 MOON-ROCKET PARTS ARRIVE FOR ASSEMBLY AT BAIKONUR COSMODROME IN SOVIET KAZAKHSTAN. THE FIRST N-1 LAUNCH IS SET FOR THE THIRD QUARTER OF 1968.
MAY 7, 1968 THE FIRST N-1 MOON ROCKET (4L) IS ERECTED ON THE LAUNCHPAD AT BAIKONUR.
JUNE 6, 1968 THE MAIDEN FLIGHT OF THE N-1 IS POSTPONED AFTER CRACKS ARE FOUND IN ITS FIRST STAGE.
SEPTEMBER 1968 ZOND 5 (RIGHT), A TEST FOR THE

CREWED MISSION, COMPLETES CIRCUMLUNAR NAVIGATION.
FEBRUARY 21, 1969 SECOND N-1 ROCKET (3L) LAUNCHED. IT CRASHES TO THE GROUND 66 SECONDS AFTER LAUNCH.
JULY 3, 1969 N-1-5L IS LAUNCHED. THE WHOLE ROCKET FALLS BACK ONTO THE LAUNCHPAD, EXPLODES, AND DESTROYS THE PAD (RIGHT, PAD AFTER CRASH).
JULY 20, 1969 APOLLO 11 LANDS ON MOON.
1970 LUNAR COSMONAUT TEAMS ARE DISBANDED.

JUNE 27, 1971 THE NEXT ATTEMPT AT AN N-1 LAUNCH ROLLS OUT OF CONTROL AND FALLS APART 48 SECONDS AFTER LAUNCH.
NOVEMBER 23, 1972 FINAL LAUNCH OF THE N-1 ROCKET (7L). IT REACHES AN ALTITUDE OF 25 MILES (40 KM), BUT AN ENGINE PIPELINE FIRE CAUSES ENGINE SHUTDOWN 107 SECONDS AFTER LAUNCH.
1974 SOVIETS END LUNAR PROGRAM.

LUNA
10–12

I n 1966, the race for the Moon was still an open contest between superpowers America and Russia. Both had successfully placed soft landers on the lunar surface, proving that machinery—and therefore humans—could stand there. The next hurdle was to place a satellite in lunar orbit. As well as commanding considerable prestige, such a mission could gather more information about the Moon's alien environment and collect pictures of potential landing sites. The Russians led the way with *Luna 10, 11,* and *12.*

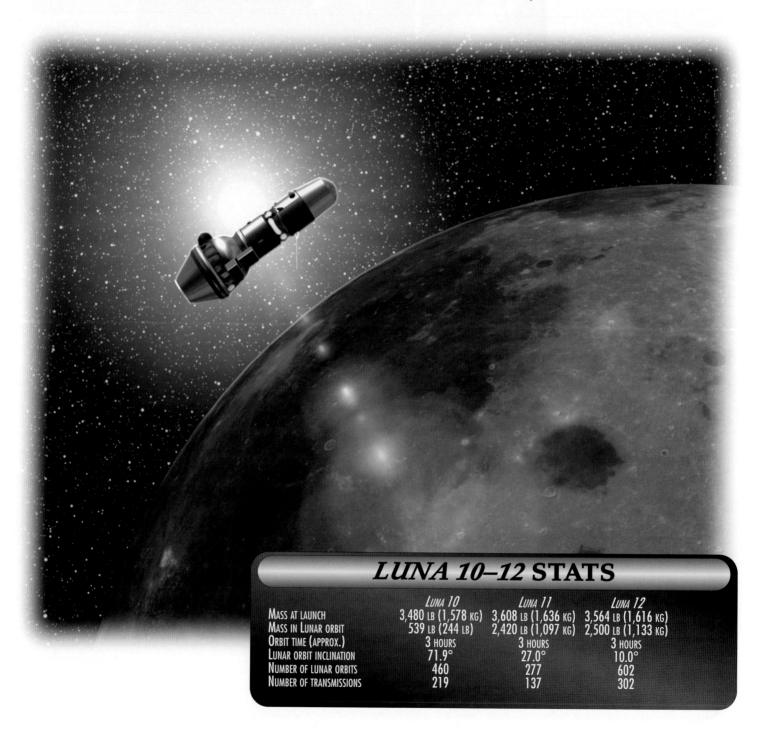

LUNA 10–12 STATS

	LUNA 10	LUNA 11	LUNA 12
MASS AT LAUNCH	3,480 LB (1,578 KG)	3,608 LB (1,636 KG)	3,564 LB (1,616 KG)
MASS IN LUNAR ORBIT	539 LB (244 LB)	2,420 LB (1,097 KG)	2,500 LB (1,133 KG)
ORBIT TIME (APPROX.)	3 HOURS	3 HOURS	3 HOURS
LUNAR ORBIT INCLINATION	71.9°	27.0°	10.0°
NUMBER OF LUNAR ORBITS	460	277	602
NUMBER OF TRANSMISSIONS	219	137	302

LUNAR LONERS

By the mid-1960s, both America and the Soviet Union had soft-landed craft on the lunar surface and were now rehearsing—in Earth orbit—the maneuvers needed to land a crewed spacecraft on the Moon. The next step was to place a satellite in lunar orbit, in order to provide more information about the lunar environment and to search for potential landing sites.

The Soviets were in the lead. In 1959, *Luna 2* became the first human-made object to hit the Moon, and in the same year *Luna 3* transmitted the first images of the Moon's far side. The USSR was also the first to achieve a soft landing with *Luna 9*.

April 3, 1966, marked yet another Soviet triumph, as *Luna 10* became the first spacecraft to orbit the Moon. Where *Luna 9* was aimed directly at the landing site, using springs and airbags to cushion the impact, *Luna 10* made the journey attached to a larger parent craft, and on approaching the Moon, fired a retrorocket that slowed it enough to be grasped by the Moon's gravity. Twenty minutes later, the orbiter was detached from the parent craft

and was released into orbit.

At 5 feet (1.5 m) long and around 18 inches (50 cm) in diameter, *Luna 10* spun at two revolutions per minute and completed one orbit every 178 minutes. Its limited payload implied that science took second place to national pride: there were devices for measuring electrical, magnetic, and radiation fields, but no camera. After fifty-six days in orbit, *Luna 10*'s batteries died and the craft fell silent.

PRESERVING THE IMAGE

By the time of the launch of *Luna 11*, five months later, the US had streaked ahead in the Moon race with *Lunar Orbiter 1*, which snapped 211 high-quality images of the Moon's surface. Despite Soviet scientists' best efforts, *Luna 11* did not match the US probe's success. After entering lunar orbit on August 28, the spacecraft appeared to vanish. The Soviets' official story was that although *Luna 11* carried an imaging camera, its mission was simply to test spacecraft

systems in lunar orbit, not to take any actual photographs. Russian sources have since revealed that in fact, *Luna 11* suffered altitude control problems: it did return images, but they were merely of empty space.

In October 1966, the Soviet news agency Tass announced that *Luna 12* would be launched to photograph the Moon's surface from lunar orbit. While it was externally similar to *Luna 11*, it carried a much larger payload than earlier Luna craft, including a camera system with a built-in "dark room" that developed, fixed, and dried the film. The developed pictures were then scanned electronically and transmitted back to Earth in a process similar to that used by fax machines.

Luna 12 achieved lunar orbit as planned on October 25, 1966. To make the most of its limited battery power, it began collecting images of the Moon's equatorial regions almost immediately.

To the delight of Soviet space scientists and Communist Party officials, *Luna 12*'s faxing system worked perfectly and images of the lunar surface were promptly beamed across the nation on Soviet television. But the tide of events had already turned in favor of the US space program. The images provided by *Luna 12* were inferior to those of *Lunar Orbiter 1*, and on January 19, 1967, the spacecraft ceased transmission. American technology was finally beginning to outpace that of its superpower rival. After *Luna 12*, the Soviet race to the Moon began to run out of steam.

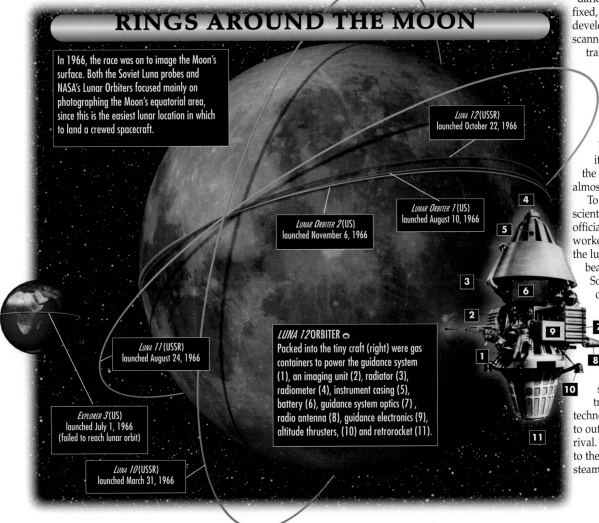

RINGS AROUND THE MOON

In 1966, the race was on to image the Moon's surface. Both the Soviet Luna probes and NASA's Lunar Orbiters focused mainly on photographing the Moon's equatorial area, since this is the easiest lunar location in which to land a crewed spacecraft.

Luna 12 (USSR)
launched October 22, 1966

Lunar Orbiter 1 (US)
launched August 10, 1966

Lunar Orbiter 2 (US)
launched November 6, 1966

Luna 11 (USSR)
launched August 24, 1966

Explorer 3 (US)
launched July 1, 1966
(failed to reach lunar orbit)

Luna 10 (USSR)
launched March 31, 1966

LUNA 12 ORBITER Packed into the tiny craft (right) were gas containers to power the guidance system (1), an imaging unit (2), radiator (3), radiometer (4), instrument casing (5), battery (6), guidance system optics (7), radio antenna (8), guidance electronics (9), altitude thrusters, (10) and retrorocket (11).

RANGER AND SURVEYOR

Back in May 1961, when President John F. Kennedy gave the go-ahead to land a man on the Moon, no one knew much about the lunar surface. Was it solid rock or was it covered in treacherous moondust, a quicksand that could swallow an entire spacecraft and its crew? NASA had to know. From 1961 through 1968, the robot Ranger and Surveyor missions were launched to find the answers to the questions that perplexed Apollo planners. These little spacecraft blazed the trail for the first humans on the Moon.

LUNAR LANDING SITES

Mission	Latitude	Longitude	Mission	Latitude	Longitude
Ranger 4	15.5° S	130.5° W	Surveyor 1	2.4° S	43.3° W
Ranger 6	9.39° N	21.51° E	Surveyor 2	5.5° N	12.0° W
Ranger 7	10.35° S	20.58° W	Surveyor 3	3.0° N	23.3° W
Ranger 8	2.6° N	24.7° E	Surveyor 4	0.4° N	1.33° W
Ranger 9	13.3° S	3.0° W	Surveyor 5	1.5° N	23.2° E
			Surveyor 6	0.53° N	1.4° W
			Surveyor 7	40.9° S	11.5° W

MOON PROBED

During the Mercury flights of the early 1960s, when US astronauts first ventured into space, NASA was already aiming for the Moon. Its Ranger spacecraft were designed to crash headlong into our nearest neighbor, beaming back progressively better pictures as they hurtled toward the surface. But the early lunar missions were far less successful than Project Mercury. The first two Rangers, launched in 1961, failed to leave Earth orbit. The following year, *Ranger 3, 4,* and *5* also ended in failure. *Ranger 3* and *5* missed the Moon completely and *Ranger 4* tumbled uselessly onto its surface. *Ranger 6* reached the Moon successfully in 1964, but was unable to send back any images because its cameras were faulty.

Success finally came later that year with *Ranger 7*, which collected pictures of the northern basin of the Sea of Clouds during the last 20 minutes before impact. It returned 4,316 images, and the last of them, taken just before the craft

struck the Moon at around 5,800 mph (9,344 kmh), were one thousand times better than any that had been taken from Earth. The views showed the maria (seas) of the Moon as relatively smooth and similar to lava flows on Earth.

Two further missions, *Rangers 8* and *9* in 1965, also made precision flights and sent back thousands more close-up images. *Ranger 8* aimed for the Sea of Tranquillity, later the site of the first human steps on the Moon, while *Ranger 9* headed for the hills. It relayed images of the Alphonsus crater in the southern highlands, an area thought to have once been volcanically active. *Ranger 9*'s impact on the lunar surface brought the series to a successful close.

CLOSE-UP VIEW

The next objective was to soft-land on the Moon and take close-up images of the lunar surface. The first craft sent to do this, *Surveyor 1*, landed only 8.7 miles (14 km) off-target in June

1966 and sent back panoramic views of the landscape. Over the next two years, it was followed by six more Surveyors, not all of which were as successful.

Mission Control lost contact with *Surveyor 2*, when a thruster failure caused it to tumble out of control onto the Moon, and with *Surveyor 4*, just minutes before touchdown. But *Surveyor 3, 5, 6,* and *7* all made it safely to the

lunar surface. They provided a mass of information, both from their cameras and from onboard instruments that sampled and analyzed the lunar surface. Among their detailed findings was the reassuring confirmation that the surface of the Moon was similar to that of fine-grained soil on Earth and would pose no problem to crewed Moon landings.

NASA RANGERS

AUGUST 23, 1961 *RANGER 1* FAILS TO LEAVE EARTH ORBIT.
NOVEMBER 18, 1961 *RANGER 2* FAILS TO LEAVE EARTH ORBIT.
JANUARY 26, 1962 *RANGER 3* IS LAUNCHED BUT MISSES THE MOON BY MORE THAN 22,800 MILES (36,700 KM).
APRIL 23, 1962 *RANGER 4* IS LAUNCHED BUT FAILS TO RETURN ANY DATA.
OCTOBER 18, 1962 *RANGER 5* IS LAUNCHED BUT MISSES THE MOON BY 450 MILES (720 KM).
JANUARY 30, 1964 *RANGER 6* IS LAUNCHED BUT FAILS TO TRANSMIT ANY IMAGES.
JULY 28, 1964 *RANGER 7* IS LAUNCHED. IT IS THE FIRST US PROBE TO PHOTOGRAPH THE MOON (RIGHT).
FEBRUARY 17, 1965 *RANGER 8* LAUNCHED; 3 DAYS LATER, IT SENDS ITS LAST PICTURE FROM A HEIGHT OF 2,100 FEET (640 M).
MARCH 21, 1965

RANGER 9 SETS OFF FOR THE CRATER ALPHONSUS, WHERE IT IMPACTS SUCCESSFULLY.
MAY 30, 1966 *SURVEYOR 1* IS LAUNCHED ON A SUCCESSFUL SOFT-LANDING MISSION. ON JUNE 2, THE PROBE SETTLES GENTLY ON THE FLOOR OF THE CRATER FLAMSTEED.
SEPTEMBER 20, 1966 *SURVEYOR 2* IS LAUNCHED BUT CRASHES INTO THE MOON INSTEAD OF MAKING A SOFT-LANDING.
APRIL 20, 1967 *SURVEYOR 3* LANDS SUCCESSFULLY IN THE MOON'S OCEAN OF STORMS.
JULY 14, 1967 *SURVEYOR 4* IS LAUNCHED BUT RADIO CONTACT IS LOST EN ROUTE TO THE MOON.
SEPTEMBER 11, 1967 *SURVEYOR 5* LANDS IN THE SEA OF TRANQUILITY.
NOVEMBER 10, 1967 *SURVEYOR 6* LANDS SAFELY — THEN "HOPS" 25 YARDS (23 M) ON ITS THRUSTERS.
JANUARY 10, 1968 *SURVEYOR 7* LANDS IN THE CRATER TYCHO, FAR FROM THE POTENTIAL APOLLO SITES.

RANGER AND SURVEYOR

HARD PUNCHER
Ranger 7 carried six TV cameras, two with 25-mm wide-angle lenses and the other four with 75-mm lenses. It weighed nearly 800 pounds (363 kg), the span of its solar panels was about 15 feet (4.6 m), and it was nearly 12 feet (3.7 m) high.

SOFT LANDER
Surveyor 3 (shown here) weighed about 665 pounds (302 kg) and its equipment included a TV camera and soil sampler. The Surveyor craft were all of the same basic design, but the scientific instruments they carried varied from one mission to another.

THE FINAL COUNTDOWN
Ranger 8 beamed back these pictures (right) in the last 9 seconds before it hit the surface of the Moon at almost 6,000 mph (10,000 kmh).

MOON BUGS

DURING THE APOLLO 12 MISSION IN NOVEMBER 1969, ASTRONAUTS PETE CONRAD AND ALAN BEAN VISITED *SURVEYOR 3* AND REMOVED SOME PIECES OF IT FOR ANALYSIS. BACK ON EARTH, RESEARCHERS FOUND EARTH BACTERIA IN A PIECE OF PLASTIC FOAM FROM INSIDE *SURVEYOR'S* TV CAMERA. THESE WERE THOUGHT TO HAVE BEEN IN THE FOAM SINCE BEFORE *SURVEYOR* WAS LAUNCHED; THEY SURVIVED FOR ALMOST THREE YEARS ON THE LUNAR SURFACE.

T–9 SECONDS
12 miles (19 km) above the surface of the Moon.

T–5 SECONDS
6.8 miles (11 km) above the surface of the Moon.

T–0.7 SECONDS
Just under 5,000 feet (1,524 m) to final lunar impact.

APOLLO TEST
FLIGHTS

The mandate of the Apollo program—to put a man on the Moon by the end of the 1960s—demanded a huge leap forward in spacecraft technology. To meet the goal, NASA devised the Saturn rocket family. Uncrewed missions were carried out to test Apollo before the US made a final commitment to sending astronauts toward the lunar target. On the whole, the missions were successful: Mission Control was able to finesse some useful data out of the technical glitches that occurred. But on the fourth test mission—the first to involve a crew of three, these glitches were to turn deadly.

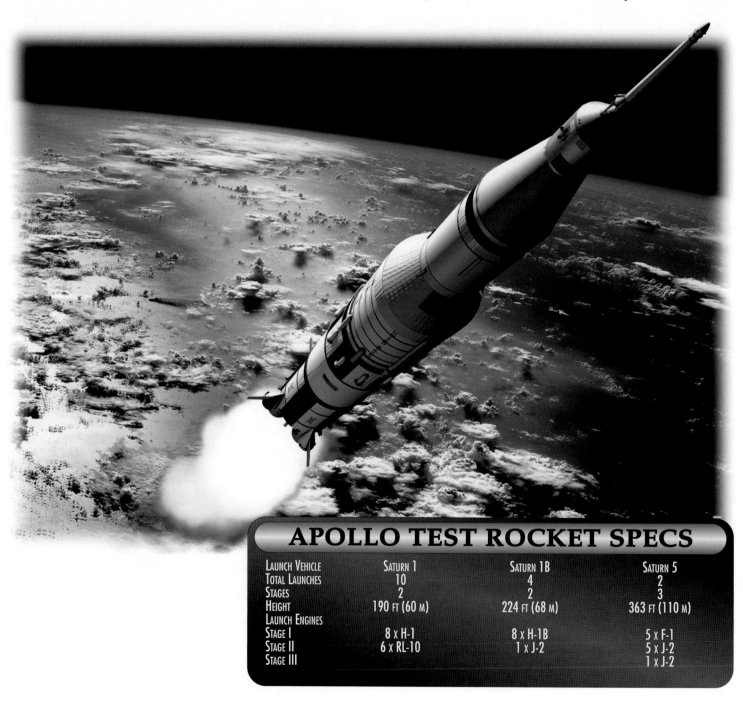

APOLLO TEST ROCKET SPECS

Launch Vehicle	Saturn 1	Saturn 1B	Saturn 5
Total Launches	10	4	2
Stages	2	2	3
Height	190 ft (60 m)	224 ft (68 m)	363 ft (110 m)
Launch Engines			
Stage I	8 x H-1	8 x H-1B	5 x F-1
Stage II	6 x RL-10	1 x J-2	5 x J-2
Stage III			1 x J-2

APOLLO MISSIONS 1–6

AS 201–3
These three flights on Saturn 1B rockets (AS-201, left) tested the Apollo module. The rocket's second stage became the third stage of the Saturn 5 rocket that would take the Apollo craft from Earth up to lunar orbit.

APOLLO 1
During a test atop an empty Saturn 1B rocket, a spark from faulty wiring ignited a fire that burned out of control in the oxygen-rich capsule (left). NASA astronauts Gus Grissom, Ed White, and Roger Chaffee died in the accident.

APOLLO 4
The first launch of the new Saturn 5 launcher was an unqualified success. Its command module endured temperatures of 5,000°F (2,800°C) before splashing down, scalded, in the Pacific Ocean (left).

The fully equipped Saturn 5 launch vehicle (left) towered 140 feet (43 m) over its predecessor, the Saturn 1B rocket (below). Four Apollo test flights flew in a Saturn 1B; two used the Moon-bound Saturn 5.

APOLLO 5
The last Saturn 1B rocket used in an Apollo mission had an oddly shaped cargo (shown above). This mission tested only the ascent and descent stages of the Lunar Module without a Command/Service Module.

TRIED & TESTED

The six test flights for the Apollo mission examined the hardware for the main stages of the Apollo lunar mission, from launch to stage separation to space maneuvers. The first three missions—AS-201, 202, and 203—launched in 1966 on a Saturn 1B rocket. These missions also checked the separation of the stages of the launcher, their electrical systems and parts of the spacecraft, including the Command Module (CM) for launch and reentry, the Service Module (SM) for orbiting around the Moon, and the Lunar Module (LM).

Planned as the first of a series of crewed test flights in Earth orbit, Apollo 1 ended in tragedy on the launchpad in January 1967. A flash fire in the Apollo 1 capsule killed the three astronauts and grounded the Apollo crewed missions for twenty-one months.

The rest of the test flights were uncrewed. Ten months after Apollo 1, the Apollo 4 Command and Service Module (CSM) was sent into Earth orbit on the new, huge Saturn 5 rocket. Apollo 4 reached a height of 11,000 miles (17,700 km) and reentered the atmosphere at 24,900 mph (40,000 kmh).

Apollo's final Saturn 1B mission in late January 1968 was the first—and only—test launch of the Lunar Module. Once in orbit, the Apollo 5 Lunar Module separated from the second stage of the Saturn launcher. After checking the onboard systems, the descent engine was fired up for a mock lunar landing. Four seconds later, onboard systems cut the engine off. A built-in safety system had detected that the engine was not firing powerfully enough, aborted the descent, and decoupled the ascent stage of the Lunar Module.

ON TO PLAN B

Although NASA engineers did not obtain data on the Lunar Module's descent engine, they did learn that their backup safety systems worked flawlessly.

The last Apollo test flight, in April 1968, did not go so smoothly. The first stage was wrenched back and forth by sloshing rocket fuel. Then two of the second-stage engines shut down, forcing the Service Module to ignite to accelerate the spacecraft to escape velocity. Although the spacecraft did not have enough fuel to reach the planned 7-mile-per-second (11 kms) reentry speed, it did allow NASA to test its contingency procedures. Now the ground was cleared for crewed tests.

MISSION DIARY: APOLLO TEST FLIGHTS

MAY 25, 1961 PRESIDENT KENNEDY COMMITS TO A MANNED LUNAR LANDING WITHIN THE DECADE.
NOVEMBER 7, 1963 FIRST OF SIX FLIGHT TESTS OF APOLLO LAUNCH ESCAPE SYSTEM ON TEST ROCKET.
JANUARY 29, 1964 FIRST ORBITAL FLIGHT OF SATURN 1.
MAY 28, 1964 FIRST FLIGHT OF CM TO PROVE COMPATIBILITY WITH SATURN 1.
SEPTEMBER 18 1964 THIRD ORBITAL FLIGHT OF SATURN 1 ROCKET, PREDECESSOR OF SATURN 1B.
JANUARY 20, 1966 FIRST FLIGHT-RATED APOLLO CAPSULE ON SIXTH AND FINAL LITTLE JOE ABORT TEST.
FEBRUARY 26, 1966 FIRST SUBORBITAL FLIGHT OF SATURN 1B WITH CSM INSTALLED.

JULY 5, 1966 FIRST ORBITAL FLIGHT OF SATURN 1B.
JANUARY 27, 1967 APOLLO 1 FIRE KILLS CREW OF FIRST MANNED ORBITAL TEST OF APOLLO ON SATURN 1B.
NOVEMBER 9, 1967 FIRST UNMANNED LAUNCH OF SATURN 5 — APOLLO 4 MISSION — WITH MOCK LUNAR MODULE; PHOTOGRAPHS THE EARTH FROM 11,000 MILES (17,000 KM).
JANUARY 22, 1968 FIRST UNMANNED LAUNCH OF LM ON SATURN 1B ROCKET.
APRIL 4, 1968 SECOND UNMANNED LAUNCH OF SATURN 5: APOLLO 6 SPLASHES DOWN SAFELY (RIGHT).

OCTOBER 1968 FIRST MANNED APOLLO CSM FLIGHT: THE APOLLO 7 MISSION.
DECEMBER 1968 FIRST MANNED SATURN 5 FLIGHT: APOLLO 8.
MARCH 1969 FIRST APOLLO LAUNCH OF SATURN 5 COMPLETE WITH LM (APOLLO 9).
JULY 1969 LUNAR LANDING: APOLLO 11.

APOLLO COMMAND MODULE

Apollo's Command Module took men to the Moon—and brought them back again. Built to house the crew during launch; provide them with air, food, and water for the journey; and serve as a base of operations during lunar landings, the tiny craft also had to survive the rigors of reentry into the Earth's atmosphere with little more than a heat shield for brakes. The demands on it to return its crew members safely were extraordinary. Yet over nine lunar voyages and two Earth orbital missions, the Command Module never failed its passengers, even when it was feared the worst might happen.

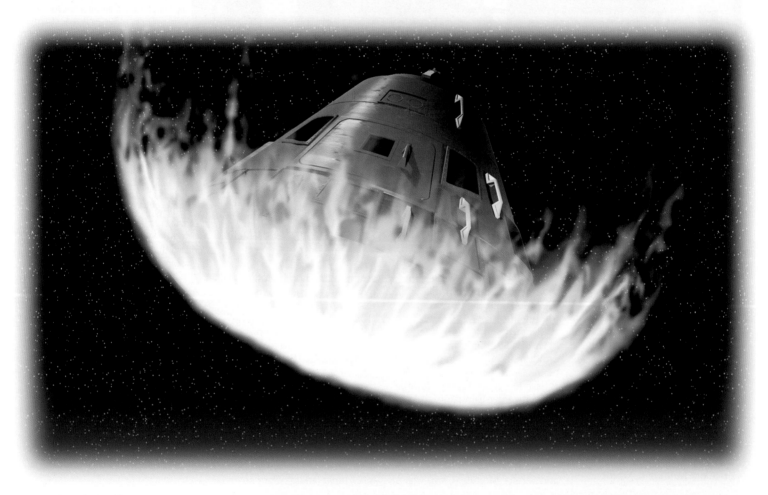

APOLLO CM SPECS

PRIME CONTRACTOR	NORTH AMERICAN AVIATION	ELECTRICAL EQUIPMENT	1,550 LB (703 KG)
CREW	THREE	COMMUNICATIONS SYSTEMS	225 LB (102 KG)
HABITABLE VOLUME	210 CU FT (5.9 M³)	NAVIGATION EQUIPMENT	1,100 LB (499 KG)
LENGTH	10 FT 6 IN (3.2 M)	ENVIRONMENTAL CONTROLS	450 LB (204 KG)
DIAMETER	12 FT 10 INCHES (3.9 M)	CREW SEATS AND PROVISIONS	550 LB (249 KG)
OVERALL MASS	12,800 LB (5,800 KG)	RECOVERY EQUIPMENT	550 LB (249 KG)
HEAT SHIELD	1,900 LB (861 KG)	MISCELLANEOUS CONTINGENCY	450 LB (204 KG)
THRUSTER SYSTEM	900 LB (408 KG)		
PROPELLANTS	175 LB (79 KG)		

SPACE WOMB

Constructed from two million separate components, the three-person Apollo Command Module (CM) was an incredibly complex machine by any standards—let alone those of the 1960s. Its task was to act as mother ship during the Moon landing missions. Out of the crew of three, one astronaut stayed in the CM during lunar orbit; the other two traveled to the surface in a separate landing craft.

The CM's cramped interior included instruments, navigation computers, and life-support equipment designed with the experience gained from the earlier Mercury and Gemini programs. However, the outer shape of the craft required a totally radical approach.

For safety's sake, NASA planners insisted that a CM returning from the Moon had to be capable of surviving reentry without using a rocket engine to slow it down beforehand. This was in case something went wrong with Apollo's propulsion systems during the mission. Because of its return trajectory across a quarter of a million miles of space, the CM would hit the Earth's atmosphere at a colossal 25,000 mph (40,000 kmh). This was 7,000 mph (11,000 kmh) faster than previous Mercury or Gemini craft returning from missions in Earth orbit.

Apollo CM designers Maxime Faget and Caldwell Johnson created a cone-shaped craft with a blunt heat shield, similar in some ways to earlier capsules, but with a smoother exterior. Then a lucky accident helped them improve the shape. The diameter of the upper stage of the Saturn 5 rocket under the CM was cut by 2 inches (5 cm).

SMOOTH SHAPE

Faget and Johnson decided to round off the edge of the blunt heat shield at the base, so the CM would fit on top of the rocket stage. The result was more aerodynamic than expected, and this new shape turned out to be a crucial benefit.

The CM had to be controllable in the air as well as in space. As the module plunged back into the atmosphere, air resistance pushed up against the heat shield. If the angle of entry was incorrect by a fraction of a degree, the craft would bounce off the atmosphere and back into space, like a flat stone skimming across the surface of a pond. But if the entry was too steep, the CM would burn to a crisp. The rounded edge allowed the CM to behave like a fat aircraft wing. The astronauts could control the exact angle of approach with twelve tiny thrusters.

In 1970, the CM's engineering saved the day, as well as the lives of the crew. When Apollo 13's oxygen tank exploded, the craft lost almost all its power. In the chill of interstellar space, sweat from the astronauts soon condensed on interior surfaces such as the instrument panel. But when the astronauts turned on the power for crucial last maneuvers, there were no electrical shorts that could have stranded them. The CM brought the astronauts back to Earth.

INSIDE THE CM

COCKPIT
CM Pilot Vance Brand (left) at the controls during the 1975 Apollo-Soyuz Test Project, during which the CM docked with the Soviet craft via a special docking adapter.

The Apollo CM consisted of an outer shell and heat shield, and an interior capsule with room for three crewmembers, plus instruments, instrument panels, batteries, and a small amount of storage space.

- crew compartment heat shield
- honeycomb-construction aluminum wall
- control panel instruments
- batteries, computers, and flight equipment
- CO_2 absorbers
- storage
- docking probe
- parachute ejector
- parachute
- pitch thruster
- rendezvous window
- Apollo hatch (removed)
- yaw thrusters
- drinking water tank
- heat shield lip
- liquid waste pipe
- roll thrusters
- waste water pipe
- environmental control systems
- support strut
- pitch thrusters

UP TOP
Above the CM is a solid-fuel rocket that pulls the CM free of the Saturn 5 rocket if the launch goes wrong.

HARD EVIDENCE

THE CENTRAL SHIP
On the Apollo lunar missions, the combined Command Module and lunar-booster Service Module (CSM) orbited the Moon, while the Lunar Module (LM) detached and descended to the surface. After their moonwalk, the landing crew blasted back into lunar orbit in the upper stage of the LM, docked with the CSM, and reentered through the CM's docking port (shown above). The Service Module's engine was then fired for the return journey home, leaving the module itself to be jettisoned shortly before reentry.

TRIAL BY FIRE
The CM was enveloped in an asbestos/epoxy resin heat shield. The mixture was squeezed into a honeycomb layer on the CM's skin, where it hardened like glue and was covered with foil. The shield slowly burned away during reentry, staining the skin (above left).

APOLLO LUNAR MODULE

T he Apollo Lunar Module was the first vehicle designed to operate purely in the vacuum of space. It was never intended to survive reentry into the Earth's atmosphere. Unlike the main Apollo crew capsule, it had no need for an aerodynamic shape or heat shielding. Instead, its priority was to be light and easily maneuverable. Most of its outer skin was nothing more than lightweight metallic foil, and even the small two-person crew compartment could have been punctured easily. This fragile, bug-like machine was created for a very specialized task—landing astronauts on the Moon.

LUNAR LANDER

Weight	9,180 lb (4,163 kg) dry; 32,331 lb (14,665 kg) fueled	Width	31 ft 2 in (9.5 m) (legs extended)
Height	22 ft 11 in (7 m)	Descent Stage Engine	1,050–9,870 lb (5-43 kN)
Width	14 ft 1 in (4.2 m) (legs stowed position)	Burn Time	15 min 10 sec
		Ascent Stage Engine	3,500 lb (15 kN)
		Burn Time	7 min 40 sec

LUNAR DELIVERY

President John F. Kennedy pledged to the nation in 1961 that a lunar landing would be undertaken within the next ten years. NASA mission planners, influenced by the ideas of the German-born rocket engineer Wernher von Braun, conceived a spacecraft called "Apollo" to touch down tail-first on the Moon and then blast off back to Earth at the end of its mission.

Other designers, led by NASA engineer John Houbolt, thought this was the wrong approach. If Apollo had to carry fuel for its return to Earth, plus reentry heat shielding and parachutes for splashdown, why must it take all this bulky equipment to the lunar surface? It would just have to be lifted off again, imposing a serious weight penalty on the design.

NASA agreed, and in 1962 the emerging Apollo concept was split into two distinct components: a Command-Service Module (CSM) and a detachable Lunar Module (LM) that would land the astronauts on the Moon. The LM had to be light enough to be launched from Earth aboard the same Saturn 5 rocket that carried the CSM. Saving weight would prove to be a very difficult challenge for the LM's designers.

Once the spacecraft was successfully in orbit around the Moon, two astronauts clambered aboard the LM for the landing. The third remained aboard the CSM to monitor systems and rendezvous with the LM when it returned from the lunar surface.

The LM consisted of two sections. On completion of its lunar surface operations, the landing legs, rocket engine, and empty fuel tanks in the lower descent stage were abandoned to save weight. Only the compact crew module, the ascent stage, lifted off for the return trip, using the main fuel tank and engine. After making a rendezvous with the CSM in lunar orbit, the entire ascent stage was thrown away altogether, saving yet more weight, and leaving just the CSM for the voyage back to earth.

The greatest danger was that the two astronauts in the ascent stage might not be able to locate the CSM in the vastness of space after their ascent from the Moon. Scientists at the Massachusetts Institute of Technology (MIT) designed a computerized navigation system with a radar altimeter. This sophisticated system solved the problem with pinpoint accuracy.

Between 1969 and 1972, the LM performed flawlessly. It flew nine crewed missions to the Moon and back, carried out an Earth orbital test, a lunar practice descent, six touchdowns, and one incredible rescue—that of Apollo 13.

FULL HOUSE

THE LM CABIN'S INTERIOR WAS SO CRAMPED THAT THE ASTRONAUTS HAD TO STAND UP DURING FLIGHT. EVEN DURING REST PERIODS ON THE MOON, THEY FOUND IT IMPOSSIBLE TO LIE DOWN COMFORTABLY BECAUSE THE ASCENT ENGINE COVER OCCUPIED MOST OF THE FLOOR.

FLYING LLRV

APOLLO ASTRONAUTS TRAINED ON A JET-POWERED LUNAR LANDING RESEARCH VEHICLE (LLRV) NICKNAMED THE "FLYING BEDSTEAD." THE LLRV WAS VERY DIFFICULT TO CONTROL: NEIL ARMSTRONG CRASHED ONE WHILE TRAINING FOR HIS MOON-LANDING MISSION AND HAD TO USE HIS EJECTION SEAT TO ESCAPE UNHARMED.

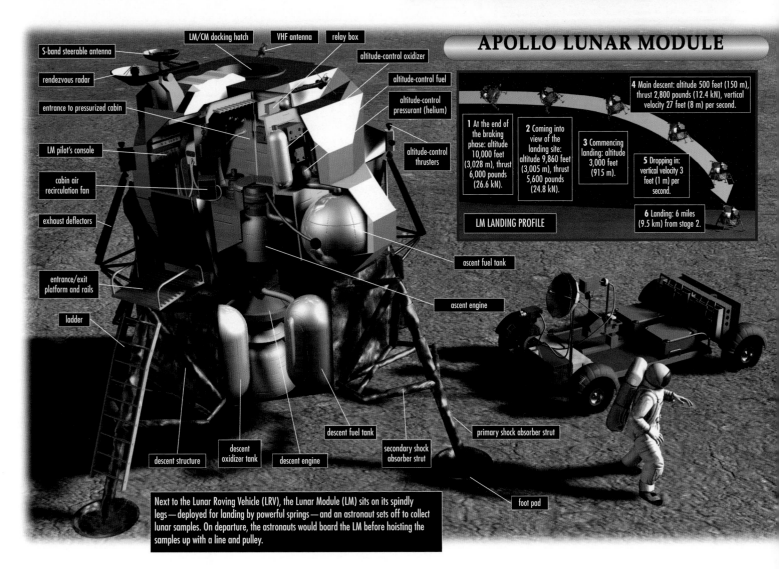

APOLLO LUNAR MODULE

S-band steerable antenna
LM/CM docking hatch
VHF antenna
relay box
rendezvous radar
altitude-control oxidizer
entrance to pressurized cabin
altitude-control fuel
altitude-control pressurant (helium)
LM pilot's console
altitude-control thrusters
cabin air recirculation fan
exhaust deflectors
entrance/exit platform and rails
ascent fuel tank
ladder
ascent engine
descent fuel tank
descent structure
descent oxidizer tank
descent engine
secondary shock absorber strut
primary shock absorber strut
foot pad

LM LANDING PROFILE

1 At the end of the braking phase: altitude 10,000 feet (3,028 m), thrust 6,000 pounds (26.6 kN).

2 Coming into view of the landing site: altitude 9,860 feet (3,005 m), thrust 5,600 pounds (24.8 kN).

3 Commencing landing: altitude 3,000 feet (915 m).

4 Main descent: altitude 500 feet (150 m), thrust 2,800 pounds (12.4 kN), vertical velocity 27 feet (8 m) per second.

5 Dropping in: vertical velocity 3 feet (1 m) per second.

6 Landing: 6 miles (9.5 km) from stage 2.

Next to the Lunar Roving Vehicle (LRV), the Lunar Module (LM) sits on its spindly legs—deployed for landing by powerful springs—and an astronaut sets off to collect lunar samples. On departure, the astronauts would board the LM before hoisting the samples up with a line and pulley.

APOLLO 8

The crew of Apollo 8 were the first three humans to break the bonds of Earth's gravity and travel to another world. Their six-day journey included twenty hours in orbit around the Moon. For NASA, the successful mission represented another step toward a lunar landing before 1970. But as the astronauts circled the Moon on Christmas Eve 1968, transmitting their descriptions of the lunar surface to a fascinated television and radio audience around the world, the Apollo 8 mission made history in its own right.

APOLLO 8 FACTS

CREW	FRANK BORMAN, COMMANDER
	JAMES A. LOVELL, LUNAR MODULE PILOT (NAVIGATOR)
	WILLIAM A. ANDERS, COMMAND MODULE PILOT (FLIGHT ENGINEER)
LAUNCH	7:51 A.M. EST, DECEMBER 21, 1968, KENNEDY SPACE CENTER
VEHICLE	SATURN 5 ROCKET; FIRST CREWED LAUNCH OF A SATURN 5

EARTH ORBITAL ALTITUDE	115 MILES
TRANSLUNAR INJECTION BURN	DECEMBER 21, 10:42 A.M. EST
LUNAR ORBIT INSERTION	DECEMBER 24, 4:59 A.M. EST
MAXIMUM ALTITUDE ABOVE EARTH	235,000 MILES (378,000 KM)
CLOSEST APPROACH TO THE MOON	69 MILES (111 KM)
DURATION OF FLIGHT	6 DAYS, 3 HOURS, 1 MINUTE

LUNARWATCHER

Astronaut Frank Borman and his crew, Jim Lovell and Bill Anders, were training for an Apollo flight test in Earth orbit in August 1968. But then CIA intelligence revealed that the Soviets were preparing to send a Soyuz spacecraft on a trip around the Moon.

NASA was determined not to be beaten to the Moon. They knew the lunar module (LM) remained in production. But the Saturn vehicle and the command module would be tested in orbit in October, and if all went well, Apollo 8 could orbit the Moon in December, without the LM. Borman told his crewmates they had new orders: they were going to the Moon for Christmas.

The watching world was captivated as the first flight to the Moon lifted off on December 22. After two Earth orbits, Capcom Michael Collins gave the historic order: "Apollo 8, you are Go for TLI." Translunar injection, or TLI, was the engine burn that sent Apollo to the Moon.

CHRISTMAS PRESENT

In the early hours of Christmas Eve, after nearly three days in space, Apollo 8 fired its engine to decelerate, and the Moon's gravity pulled the spacecraft into its orbit. As soon as they could, the crew radioed their impressions of the surface. "Essentially gray, no color… Looks like plaster of Paris," said Lovell. Anders chipped in, "Or sort of a grayish beach sand." The crew described and photographed the features of the far side of the Moon, which had never before been seen by human eyes.

On the fourth revolution, the astronauts were startled by the beautiful sight of Earth rising above the lunar horizon. And on the ninth orbit, Apollo 8 made its famous Christmas Eve television broadcast to the people of Earth, the planet Lovell called "a grand oasis in the big vastness of space." Twenty hours after reaching lunar orbit, Apollo 8 headed back to Earth and straight into the history books.

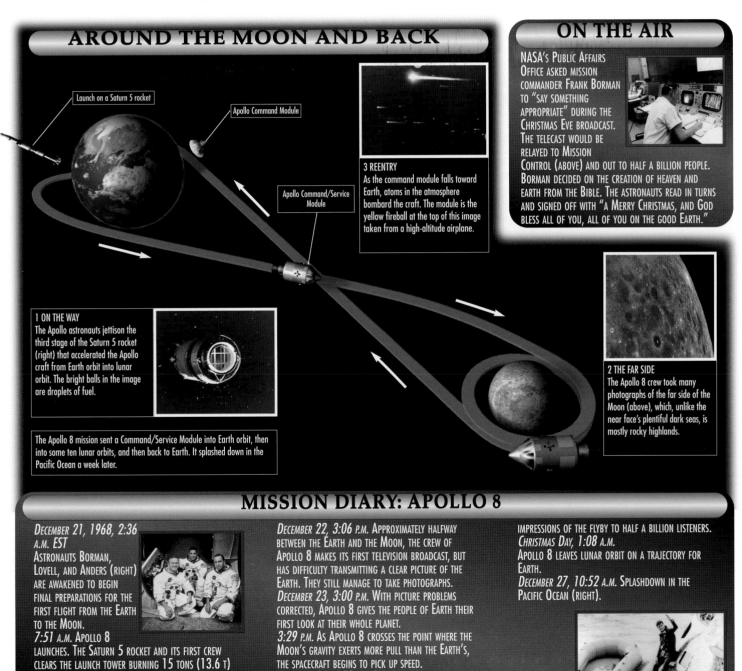

AROUND THE MOON AND BACK

Launch on a Saturn 5 rocket

Apollo Command Module

Apollo Command/Service Module

3 REENTRY
As the command module falls toward Earth, atoms in the atmosphere bombard the craft. The module is the yellow fireball at the top of this image taken from a high-altitude airplane.

1 ON THE WAY
The Apollo astronauts jettison the third stage of the Saturn 5 rocket (right) that accelerated the Apollo craft from Earth orbit into lunar orbit. The bright balls in the image are droplets of fuel.

The Apollo 8 mission sent a Command/Service Module into Earth orbit, then into some ten lunar orbits, and then back to Earth. It splashed down in the Pacific Ocean a week later.

ON THE AIR

NASA's Public Affairs Office asked mission commander Frank Borman to "say something appropriate" during the Christmas Eve broadcast. The telecast would be relayed to Mission Control (above) and out to half a billion people. Borman decided on the creation of heaven and earth from the Bible. The astronauts read in turns and signed off with "a Merry Christmas, and God bless all of you, all of you on the good Earth."

2 THE FAR SIDE
The Apollo 8 crew took many photographs of the far side of the Moon (above), which, unlike the near face's plentiful dark seas, is mostly rocky highlands.

MISSION DIARY: APOLLO 8

December 21, 1968, 2:36 a.m. EST
Astronauts Borman, Lovell, and Anders (right) are awakened to begin final preparations for the first flight from the Earth to the Moon.
7:51 a.m. Apollo 8 launches. The Saturn 5 rocket and its first crew clears the launch tower burning 15 tons (13.6 t) of fuel per second.
10:42 a.m. Lovell pushes the translunar injection button, which ignites the Saturn 5's third stage engine and sends Apollo 8 on its way to the Moon.
11:12 a.m. The spent third stage separates.

December 22, 3:06 p.m. Approximately halfway between the Earth and the Moon, the crew of Apollo 8 makes its first television broadcast, but has difficulty transmitting a clear picture of the Earth. They still manage to take photographs.
December 23, 3:00 p.m. With picture problems corrected, Apollo 8 gives the people of Earth their first look at their whole planet.
3:29 p.m. As Apollo 8 crosses the point where the Moon's gravity exerts more pull than the Earth's, the spacecraft begins to pick up speed.
December 24, 4:59 a.m. Lovell starts the lunar orbit insertion burn. The service propulsion engine burns for 4 minutes to slow Apollo 8 and send it in an elliptical orbit around the Moon.
9:34 p.m. The crew broadcast their personal

impressions of the flyby to half a billion listeners.
Christmas Day, 1:08 a.m.
Apollo 8 leaves lunar orbit on a trajectory for Earth.
December 27, 10:52 a.m. Splashdown in the Pacific Ocean (right).

APOLLO 11

O n July 20, 1969, as the whole world held its breath, Apollo 11's lunar lander, the *Eagle*, touched down on the Moon. Later, after a few hours rest, the mission commander Neil Armstrong descended the exit ladder followed by Edwin "Buzz" Aldrin and planted the Stars and Stripes in the dust of the Sea of Tranquillity. It was the culmination of a $25 billion program started by President John F. Kennedy in 1961. Neil Armstrong and Buzz Aldrin became the first human beings ever to set foot on another world.

APOLLO 11 STATS

CREWED SPACEFLIGHT	NUMBER 33		TIME ON MOON	21 HR, 36 MIN
AMERICAN CREWED SPACEFLIGHT	NUMBER 21			
CREWED FLIGHT TO THE MOON	NUMBER 3		MASS OF LUNAR SAMPLES	48.5 LB (22 KG)
PREVIOUS CREWED FLIGHTS	APOLLO 8 AND 10 TEST MISSIONS TO THE MOON			RETURNED
			PRIOR FLIGHTS OF CREW	ARMSTRONG: *GEMINI 8*
				COLLINS: *GEMINI 10*
FLIGHT OF SATURN 5 ROCKET	NUMBER 5			ALDRIN: *GEMINI 12*
FLIGHT TIME	8 DAYS, 3 HR, 18 MIN, 35 SEC		TRANQUILLITY BASE LOCATION	MOON COORDINATES 0.68°N 23.43°E

ONE GIANT LEAP

Apollo 11 carried three astronauts, two of whom—Neil Armstrong and Buzz Aldrin—would be the first to set foot on the Moon. The third, Michael Collins, was assigned to remain in the command module, *Columbia*, taking care of business while it orbited the Moon. The mission began on July 16, 1969, with Armstrong, Aldrin, and Collins perched on top of a 363-foot (110 m) Saturn 5 rocket as 7.5 million pounds (33,350 kN) of thrust blasted them into space. Once in Earth orbit, the third and final stage of the Saturn 5 shut down. Apollo 11 then swung around the Earth and the third stage reignited to propel the craft on its three-day journey to the Moon.

On arrival in lunar orbit, Armstrong and Aldrin crawled into the landing craft, *Eagle*, which had been tucked into the top of the third stage to protect it during launch. The two spacecraft separated. Then the *Eagle*'s descent engine fired to propel it toward the landing site in the Sea of Tranquillity. As the *Eagle* made its final approach, Armstrong spotted that it was overshooting the landing site and prepared to abort. Mission Control in Houston ordered him to continue.

GOOD JUDGMENT

As the *Eagle* prepared to land, Armstrong found that the onboard computer was steering it into a rocky crater, with potentially disastrous results. He immediately seized control and flew over the crater with less than 30 seconds of fuel left, leaving Mission Control powerless to do anything other than watch and trust in his judgment. With about 20 seconds of fuel left, the craft touched down. "Houston, Tranquillity Base here," said Armstrong. "The *Eagle* has landed."

Later, Armstrong emerged from the *Eagle*'s hatch and climbed down the exit ladder, watched by a huge worldwide TV audience. As he set foot on the Moon's surface, he uttered the famous words: "That's one small step for man, one giant leap for mankind" (actually a mistake: he meant to say "...one small step for a man...").

Aldrin then joined Armstrong on the surface, where they spent about two hours gathering rocks and deploying experiments. Then they returned to the *Eagle* and lifted off. Finally, after a delicate docking maneuver with the *Columbia* command module, Collins fired the rocket engine that would fly the crew home—and into history.

5 DOCKING
Collins took this remarkable photo of the *Eagle* ascent stage and Earthrise as the lunar module approached the *Columbia* command module in lunar orbit.

THE APOLLO 11 MISSION

6 SPLASHDOWN
Columbia splashed down beneath three parachutes 825 miles (1,327 km) southwest of Honolulu. The crew was on the deck of the recovery ship, USS *Hornet*, one hour later to be greeted by President Nixon.

3 LUNAR LANDING
"Picking up some dust," said Aldrin. "30 feet, 2½ down...faint shadow...4 forward...4 forward...drifting to the right a little...contact light...OK engine stop."

4 TAKEOFF
Lifting off at a speed of 80 feet (24 m) per second, the *Eagle* used its spent descent stage as a launchpad as it cleared the dusty, airless surface of Tranquillity Base.

1 SATURN 5
The rocket that powered the Apollo mission is the most powerful ever built in the US. At launch, its five F-1 first-stage engines gulped 5,000 gallons (19,000 l) of liquid oxygen and kerosene a second.

2 ESCAPE FROM EARTH
The Saturn 5's S4B third stage was fired to accelerate Apollo 11 to over 25,000 mph (40,000 kmh) — the escape velocity required to enable the craft to break free of the Earth's gravitational field.

MISSION DIARY: APOLLO 11

May 1961 President John F. Kennedy commits the US to putting a man on the Moon "before the decade is out." The program is named Apollo.
July 16, 1969, 9:32 a.m. EDT Apollo 11 is launched (right).
9:44 a.m. Apollo 11 enters Earth orbit.
12:22 p.m. The third stage of the Saturn 5 rocket reignites, blasting Apollo 11 out of Earth orbit and toward the Moon.
12:49 p.m. The Apollo 11 command and service

module separate, turn around, and dock with the lunar module.
July 19, 1:28 p.m. Apollo 11 goes into orbit around the Moon.
July 20, 1:46 p.m. The lunar module *Eagle* separates from the orbiting command module *Columbia*.
3:08 p.m. *Eagle* begins its powered descent.
July 20, 4:18 p.m. "The *Eagle* has landed."
10:56 p.m. Armstrong becomes the first person on the Moon.

July 21, 1:54 p.m. The *Eagle* leaves the surface of the Moon.
5:35 p.m. *Eagle* docks with *Columbia*; the crew transfer to the command module.
July 22, 12:56 a.m. *Columbia* blasts out of lunar orbit back toward Earth.
July 24, 12:51 p.m. *Columbia* and its jubilant crew members splash down safely in the Pacific Ocean (above).

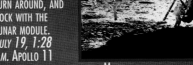

APOLLO 13

Launched on April 11, 1970, Apollo 13 was NASA's third attempt at a manned landing on the Moon. The launch itself was a low-key occasion, the press and public having already grown used to the idea of lunar exploration. But then, just over two days into the mission, the world was shocked to attention by the crew's famous radio message: "Houston...we've had a problem here." An onboard explosion had put the lives of the astronauts in serious jeopardy—along with the future of the US space program.

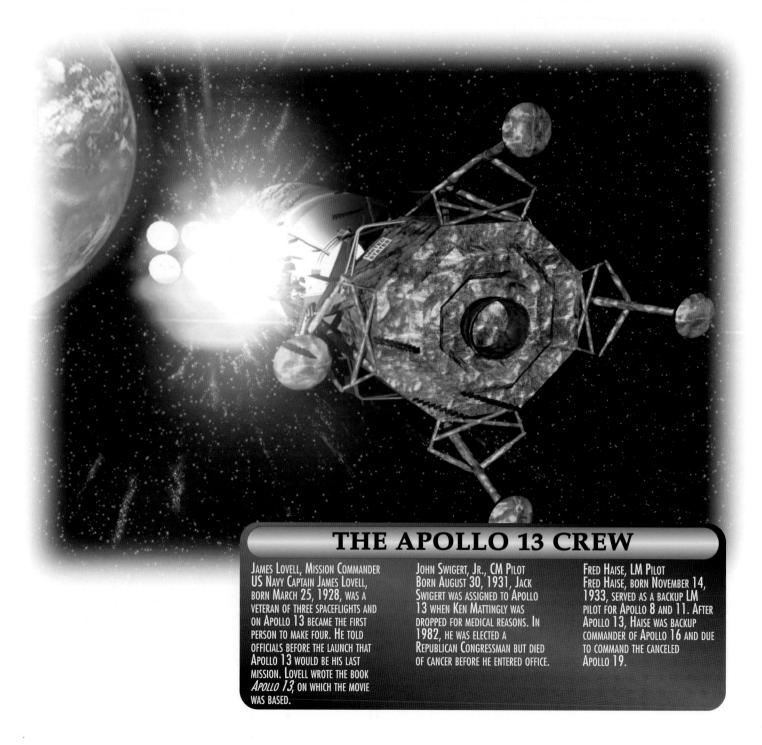

THE APOLLO 13 CREW

JAMES LOVELL, MISSION COMMANDER US NAVY CAPTAIN JAMES LOVELL, BORN MARCH 25, 1928, WAS A VETERAN OF THREE SPACEFLIGHTS AND ON APOLLO 13 BECAME THE FIRST PERSON TO MAKE FOUR. HE TOLD OFFICIALS BEFORE THE LAUNCH THAT APOLLO 13 WOULD BE HIS LAST MISSION. LOVELL WROTE THE BOOK *APOLLO 13*, ON WHICH THE MOVIE WAS BASED.

JOHN SWIGERT, JR., CM PILOT BORN AUGUST 30, 1931, JACK SWIGERT WAS ASSIGNED TO APOLLO 13 WHEN KEN MATTINGLY WAS DROPPED FOR MEDICAL REASONS. IN 1982, HE WAS ELECTED A REPUBLICAN CONGRESSMAN BUT DIED OF CANCER BEFORE HE ENTERED OFFICE.

FRED HAISE, LM PILOT FRED HAISE, BORN NOVEMBER 14, 1933, SERVED AS A BACKUP LM PILOT FOR APOLLO 8 AND 11. AFTER APOLLO 13, HAISE WAS BACKUP COMMANDER OF APOLLO 16 AND DUE TO COMMAND THE CANCELED APOLLO 19.

"HOUSTON...WE'VE HAD A PROBLEM HERE"

As their mighty Saturn 5 launch vehicle thundered into the afternoon skies above the Kennedy Space Center, Apollo 13 astronauts James Lovell, Fred Haise, and Jack Swigert began to look forward to their long journey to the Moon. But inside bay 4 of the Service Module, a fault in the number 2 oxygen tank had already turned their spacecraft into a bomb, primed and ready to blow apart.

The tank was part of the Apollo craft's fuel cell system, which produced electricity and water from hydrogen and oxygen. It contained a stirring fan, a heating element, and two thermostatic control switches. These switches were designed to operate at 28 volts, but the spacecraft's power supply had been upgraded to 65 volts. As a result, during tests in the weeks before the launch, the higher voltage caused arcing that welded the switches shut. This somehow went unnoticed. During later testing, the faulty switches allowed the temperature of the tank assembly to reach over 1,000°F (540°C), which damaged the insulation of the fan wiring.

The tank finally exploded just under 56 hours into the mission, when Apollo 13 was 205,000 miles (330,000 km) from Earth and the crew was increasing the hydrogen and oxygen pressures to keep the fuel cells functioning properly.

THE JOURNEY HOME

When the accident happened, there was a loud bang and the crew felt the craft shudder. The damaged fan wiring had shorted out, leading to a violent tank explosion that ripped a 13-foot-by-6-foot (4-m-by-1.8 m) panel out of the Service Module.

Soon, the Command Module was effectively without power, oxygen, and water. Additionally, the main engine, part of the Service Module, was completely immobilized and unresponsive.

The crew transferred from the Command Module to the Lunar Module, *Aquarius*. This tiny two-man craft became a "lifeboat," providing essential life-support systems. It also provided propulsion from its descent engine, which was fired several times to send the crew around the Moon and back to Earth. For much of the journey home, Lovell, Swigert, and Haise huddled in the cold Lunar Module, desperately conserving oxygen, water, and power. As Apollo 13 rapidly plunged back to Earth, *Aquarius* was discarded and the crew transferred back to the Command Module. This splashed down safely in the Pacific Ocean, just 4 miles (6.5 km) from the recovery ship *Iwo Jima*. The crew were not harmed by their terrifying ordeal.

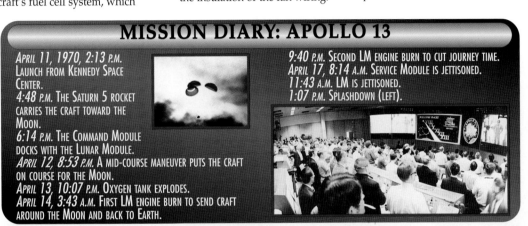

MISSION DIARY: APOLLO 13

APRIL 11, 1970, 2:13 P.M. LAUNCH FROM KENNEDY SPACE CENTER.
4:48 P.M. THE SATURN 5 ROCKET CARRIES THE CRAFT TOWARD THE MOON.
6:14 P.M. THE COMMAND MODULE DOCKS WITH THE LUNAR MODULE.
APRIL 12, 8:53 P.M. A MID-COURSE MANEUVER PUTS THE CRAFT ON COURSE FOR THE MOON.
APRIL 13, 10:07 P.M. OXYGEN TANK EXPLODES.
APRIL 14, 3:43 A.M. FIRST LM ENGINE BURN TO SEND CRAFT AROUND THE MOON AND BACK TO EARTH.

9:40 P.M. SECOND LM ENGINE BURN TO CUT JOURNEY TIME.
APRIL 17, 8:14 A.M. SERVICE MODULE IS JETTISONED.
11:43 A.M. LM IS JETTISONED.
1:07 P.M. SPLASHDOWN (LEFT).

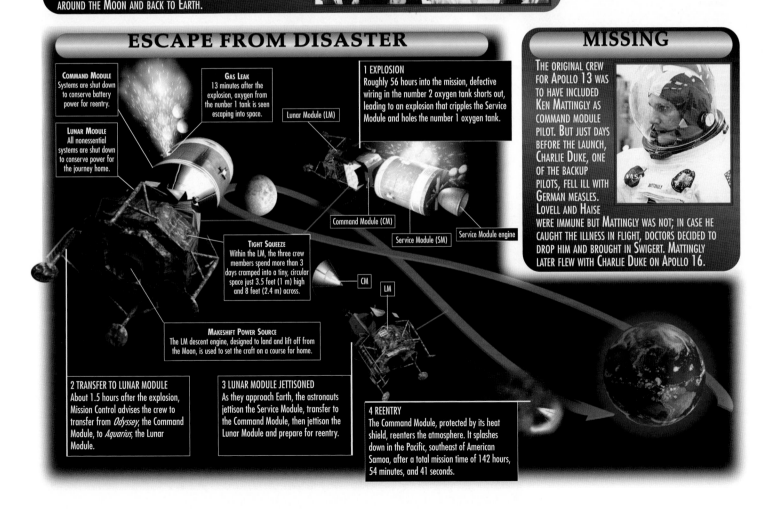

ESCAPE FROM DISASTER

COMMAND MODULE
Systems are shut down to conserve battery power for reentry.

LUNAR MODULE
All nonessential systems are shut down to conserve power for the journey home.

GAS LEAK
13 minutes after the explosion, oxygen from the number 1 tank is seen escaping into space.

Lunar Module (LM)

1 EXPLOSION
Roughly 56 hours into the mission, defective wiring in the number 2 oxygen tank shorts out, leading to an explosion that cripples the Service Module and holes the number 1 oxygen tank.

Command Module (CM)

Service Module (SM)

Service Module engine

TIGHT SQUEEZE
Within the LM, the three crew members spend more than 3 days cramped into a tiny, circular space just 3.5 feet (1 m) high and 8 feet (2.4 m) across.

CM

LM

MAKESHIFT POWER SOURCE
The LM descent engine, designed to land and lift off from the Moon, is used to set the craft on a course for home.

2 TRANSFER TO LUNAR MODULE
About 1.5 hours after the explosion, Mission Control advises the crew to transfer from *Odyssey*, the Command Module, to *Aquarius*, the Lunar Module.

3 LUNAR MODULE JETTISONED
As they approach Earth, the astronauts jettison the Service Module, transfer to the Command Module, then jettison the Lunar Module and prepare for reentry.

4 REENTRY
The Command Module, protected by its heat shield, reenters the atmosphere. It splashes down in the Pacific, southeast of American Samoa, after a total mission time of 142 hours, 54 minutes, and 41 seconds.

MISSING

THE ORIGINAL CREW FOR APOLLO 13 WAS TO HAVE INCLUDED KEN MATTINGLY AS COMMAND MODULE PILOT. BUT JUST DAYS BEFORE THE LAUNCH, CHARLIE DUKE, ONE OF THE BACKUP PILOTS, FELL ILL WITH GERMAN MEASLES. LOVELL AND HAISE WERE IMMUNE BUT MATTINGLY WAS NOT; IN CASE HE CAUGHT THE ILLNESS IN FLIGHT, DOCTORS DECIDED TO DROP HIM AND BROUGHT IN SWIGERT. MATTINGLY LATER FLEW WITH CHARLIE DUKE ON APOLLO 16.

APOLLO 14

A pollo 14 began the heavy-duty exploration of the Moon. Edgar Mitchell and Alan Shepard, America's first man in space, spent two days on the lunar surface, pushing the limits of what could safely be done. By the launch of the mission, on January 31, 1971, the Apollo program was a smoothly running machine. The Apollo 14 spacecraft had been modified to correct the failures of Apollo 13 and to extend their capabilities. But, as all engineers know, anything that can go wrong, will go wrong.

MISSION DATA

LAUNCH	JANUARY 31, 1971, 5:03 P.M. EST	MISSION DURATION	9 DAYS 2 MIN
CREW	MISSION COMMANDER ALAN SHEPARD	TIME ON MOON	33.5 HOURS
	COMMAND MODULE PILOT STUART	LUNAR TOUCHDOWN	FEBRUARY 5, 1971, 4:18 A.M. EST
	ROOSA	LUNAR LIFTOFF	FEBRUARY 6, 1:48 P.M. EST
	LUNAR MODULE PILOT EDGAR	SPLASHDOWN	FEBRUARY 9, 1971, 4:05 P.M. EST
	MITCHELL	FRA MAURO BASE	3° 40' 24" SOUTH,
TIME IN LUNAR ORBIT	67 HOURS (34 ORBITS)		17° 27' 55" WEST.

LUCKY FOURTEEN

Apollo 14 blasted off from Cape Canaveral into a cloudy and rainy afternoon sky on January 31, 1971, to become a textbook example of how to cope with minor problems. Commander and former Mercury astronaut Alan Shepard, Command Module Pilot Stuart Roosa, and Lunar Module Pilot Ed Mitchell had inherited the mission and target base of the failed Apollo 13, with extra objectives and new space techniques to try out.

They were bound for Fra Mauro, a cratered highland area that geologists hoped would provide samples of the earliest bedrock of the Moon and give clues to the early history of the Earth. They would stay longer, conduct more tests, and test the endurance of their spacesuits and themselves more than anyone had done before.

The problems that they were to face would be ironed out by the astronauts and by the well-oiled organization behind them at Mission Control. They had already modified their orbit to make up for the 40-minute launch delay caused by the bad weather.

After the spacecraft had moved into lunar orbit, Roosa maneuvered the Command Module *Kitty Hawk* to dock with the Lunar Module *Antares*, still attached to the third stage of the booster. The tiny teeth on the Lunar Module failed to engage. Two more tries were unsuccessful. By this time, engineers at Mission Control had dragged in an identical mechanism to try to find the problem. The fault remains a mystery, but on his sixth try, Roosa locked on. The mission continued, and Apollo 14 entered lunar orbit on February 4.

MOON TRACKS

Sunlight glints on tracks leading across the Moon's Fra Mauro highlands from the Lunar Module *Antares*. The tracks were made by Apollo 14's Modularized Equipment Transporter during Shepard and Mitchell's first trip away from *Antares*.

LOST
The rolling highlands of Fra Mauro made navigation difficult. Shepard and Mitchell (above, consulting a map) often lost sight of each other and had difficulty keeping a fix on landmarks.

THE FLYING RICKSHAW
An artist's impression (left) shows Shepard and Mitchell setting out on their first EVA. Shepard, on the right, is pulling the Modularized Equipment Transporter (MET), otherwise known as the "Flying Rickshaw." This two-wheeled buggy held up to 360 pounds (163 kg) of equipment, but the two astronauts sometimes found it easier to carry it than to pull it through the lunar dust.

LUNAR GOLF

As *Antares* prepared to land, Shepard and Mitchell had to reprogram its control computer while they went through their descent preparations, because the module's "abort" button was malfunctioning. To everyone's relief, their reprogramming was successful and the module touched down safely on a 7° slope only 175 feet (53 m) from its target. Shepard and Mitchell now began setting up an automated scientific laboratory. This included an instrument to measure lunar seismic activity; a series of experiments to measure charged particles near the surface; a small nuclear generator; and a station to transmit all their data to Earth. On their return to the Lunar Module, they collected some Moon rocks, but they picked up most of their geological samples during their second extravehicular activity (EVA).

Back at the Lunar Module, Shepard produced a golf ball and an improvised club. On his second swing, he claimed that the ball had gone for "miles and miles and miles." It wasn't true, but he had become the first lunar golfer. Shepard later confessed that he had tears in his eyes as he first stood on the Moon.

MISSION DIARY: APOLLO 14

JANUARY 31, 1971 APOLLO 14 CREW SUITS UP (RIGHT) FOR LAUNCH. EIGHT MINUTES BEFORE THE LAUNCH, IT IS DELAYED FOR 40 MINUTES 2 SECONDS DUE TO HEAVY CLOUDS.
JANUARY 31, 4:03 P.M. EST APOLLO 14 LIFTS OFF, CARRIED BY A SATURN 5 LAUNCHER.
FEBRUARY 5, 11:50 P.M. LUNAR MODULE *ANTARES*, CARRYING ALAN SHEPARD AND ED MITCHELL, SEPARATES FROM COMMAND MODULE *KITTY HAWK*, PILOTED BY STUART ROOSA.
FEBRUARY 5, 4:18 A.M. *ANTARES* (RIGHT) TOUCHES DOWN ON A GENTLE SLOPE IN THE HIGHLANDS NEAR THE

MOON'S FRA MAURO CRATER. THE LANDING SITE, AT LATITUDE 3° 40' 24" SOUTH AND LONGITUDE 17° 27' 55" WEST, IS ONLY 175 FEET (53 M) FROM THE PLANNED TOUCHDOWN POSITION.
FEBRUARY 5, 9:42 A.M. ALAN SHEPARD AND ED MITCHELL BEGIN THEIR FIRST MOONWALK, OR EXTRAVEHICULAR ACTIVITY (EVA), LASTING 4 HOURS 49 MINUTES.
FEBRUARY 6, 5:11 A.M. SHEPARD AND MITCHELL SET OFF ON THEIR SECOND AND FINAL EVA, LASTING 4 HOURS 35 MINUTES.

FEBRUARY 6, 1:48 P.M. AFTER 33.5 HOURS ON THE MOON, *ANTARES* LIFTS OFF FOR A RENDEZVOUS WITH *KITTY HAWK*.
FEBRUARY 9, 4:05 P.M. SPLASHDOWN AFTER 9 DAYS 2 MINUTES IN SPACE. SHEPARD, MITCHELL, AND ROOSA GO INTO QUARANTINE (ABOVE) ON USS *NEW ORLEANS*.

GLOSSARY

air lock A small room that has two doors that can be sealed tightly so that no air enters or leaves and that is used for moving between two spaces with different air pressures in a submarine or spacecraft.

arc A brightly glowing electric current that flows across an open space between two points.

astrophysics The scientific study of the physical and chemical properties and structures of stars, planets, and other objects found in space.

ballistic missile A weapon that is shot through the sky over a great distance and then falls to the ground and explodes.

booster The first stage of a multistage rocket providing thrust for the launch and the first part of the flight.

cosmonaut An astronaut in the space program of Russia or the former Soviet Union.

decompression To release or reduce the physical pressure on something.

gyroscope A wheel, used to steer something, that spins quickly and is held in a frame that allows it to tilt in any direction.

heat shield A barrier of material to protect a space capsule from heat on its entry into an atmosphere by absorbing or deflecting external heat.

infrared Producing or using rays of light that cannot be seen and that are longer than rays that produce red light.

jettison A voluntary discharge of cargo to lighten a ship's load.

lander A space vehicle that is designed to land on a celestial body, such as the Moon or a planet.

launchpad The area from which a rocket is launched.

maria Large, dark plains found on the Moon and Mars.

micrometeorite A meteorite that is so small it can pass through the Earth's atmosphere without becoming extremely heated.

moonship A spacecraft for travel to the Moon.

nose cone The pointed front end of an aircraft, rocket, or missile.

orbit To travel around something, such as a planet or the Moon, in a curved path.

orbiter A vehicle or device that travels around a planet or the Moon.

payload The things, such as passengers or bombs, that are carried by an aircraft or spacecraft.

periscope A long tube that contains lenses and mirrors and that is used to look over or around something.

radiation A kind of dangerous and powerful energy that is produced by radioactive substances and nuclear reactions.

retrorocket A reserve rocket engine (as on a spacecraft) used in decelerating.

rover A vehicle used to explore the surface of an extraterrestrial body, like the Moon or a planet.

servomotor A power-driven mechanism that supplements a primary control operated by a comparatively feeble force.

solar panel A large, flat piece of equipment that uses the Sun's light or heat to create electricity.

spectrometer An instrument used for measuring wavelengths of light spectra.

stratosphere The upper layer of the Earth's atmosphere that begins about 7 miles (11 km) above the Earth's surface and ends about 30 miles (50 km) above the Earth's surface.

thruster A small rocket engine on a spacecraft that is used to make changes in its flight path or altitude.

trajectory The curved path along which something, such as a rocket, travels through the air or through space.

translunar injection A maneuver used to accelerate a spacecraft and send it on a trajectory around the Moon.

FURTHER INFORMATION

BOOKS

Bisney, John, and J.L Pickering. *Spaceshots and Snapshots of Projects Mercury and Gemini: A Rare Photographic History*. Albuquerque, NM: University of New Mexico Press, 2015.

Bush Gibson, Karen. *Women in Space: 23 Stories of First Flights, Scientific Missions, and Gravity-Breaking Adventures*. Chicago: Chicago Review Press, 2014.

Chaikin, Andrew. *Voices from the Moon: Apollo Astronauts Describe Their Lunar Experiences*. New York: Penguin Group, 2009.

Hadfield, Chris. *You Are Here: Around the World in 92 Minutes: Photographs from the International Space Station*. New York: Little, Brown and Company, 2014.

Johnson, Michael Peter. *Mission Control: Inventing the Groundwork of Spaceflight*. Gainsville, FL: University of Florida Press, 2015.

WEBSITES

ESA: Welcome to Mir
www.esa.int/About_Us/Welcome_to_ESA/Mir_FAQs_-_Facts_and_history
Learn all about the facts and history of the Russian space station Mir.

NASA: The History of Human Spaceflight
www.nasa.gov/centers/kennedy/about/history/spacehistory_toc.html
This comprehensive website provides in-depth information on NASA's historic and future space programs.

NASA: Spot the Station
http://spotthestation.nasa.gov/sightings/#.VeRzM3hX_lI
This website allows you to track over 6,700 locations where the International Space Station is visible from at certain times.

Smithsonian National Air and Space Museum: Apollo Missions
http://airandspace.si.edu/explore-and-learn/topics/apollo/apollo-program/orbital-missions/
Read all about the Apollo missions in detail and view images from each mission.

Space.com: Moon Facts: Fun Information About the Earth's Moon
This article provides an overview of the Moon, its geological makeup, landforms, and a history of humanity's fascination with this celestial object.

INDEX

Page numbers in boldface are illustrations. Entries in boldface are glossary terms.